EPIC

Four Voices One Story

Cover art by Nelson Grice. www.nelsongriceart.com

More information is available at www.bradandjayme.com

Translated and arranged by Brad Martin

Edited by Ann Grice

Brad's Thanks

Here's to the Iron Maiden who has to be in order to stay with this driven rebel. At least it hasn't been boring.

Here's to my sons Cody, Caleb, Caius, and Cooper, and their clans. Nothing matters to me as much as you, and nothing matters without Him.

Here's to Ann and Nelson Grice – My favorite people.

Here's to Margaret Slusher who unwittingly started me down this storying path.

Here's to John, Randy, Tom, and Kim for making this possible.
Here's to Tim Samples for another set of eyes on the text and a kindred heart.
Here's to mom & dad – you raised me right.

Here's to my three invisible friends – If this makes you smile at all, it is enough for me.

Ann's Thanks

Nelson, all my love.
Thank you for your steadfast encouragement and for always making me laugh.

Brad, much gratitude.
Thank you for your commitment to excellence, and for your vision.

And to The Epic One.
Thank you. Always.

About the Authors

Brad and Jayme have been married 29 years (at the time of this writing) and together they made five sons and enjoy four grandchildren. Loving the outdoors, he translated much of *Epic* either at the stone table or on the back deck. He recently completed a Master of Arts in Teaching English at Kennesaw State University and now teaches English and coaches wrestling at North Paulding High School after spending 23 years as a Senior Pastor. He lives in Cartersville, GA and pursues God with friends. His education includes a Master of Divinity from Beeson Divinity School at Samford University, Master of Ministry in Theology from Covington Theological Seminary, and a Bachelor of Theology from the Baptizer College of Florida. You can read more about Brad and what he writes at his blog: themend.wordpress.com or connect at bradamteacher@gmail.com.

Ann Grice is a freelance writer and editor living in Alabama. She graduated summa cum laude from the University of Montevallo with a BA in English. After growing up in New Orleans, she moved to Birmingham where she met and married her high school sweetheart, Nelson Grice. They've been married for almost 26 years (2015) and have 5 children. Her fondness for detail is also illustrated in her photography where she spends her free time taking a closer look at things considered 'ordinary' and showcasing them as beautiful. You can connect with Ann on Twitter (@annmgrice) or by email at anngrice5@gmail.com.

Beginning Stuff from Brad

Before you turn the page you should be aware of what you are getting yourself into. This is not a "Christian" book. It is not a sermon. It is not a prescription for a happy life. Some will say it is not even an epic. Technically it is not an epic – a long poem. But "epic" broke out of that box some time ago. It morphed, as an epic word will do, to describe any larger-than-life hero story, true or not. Therefore, nothing could be more epic than the life of Jesus the Nazarene.

Christians say he is "fully God and fully man." Islam claims he is "a messenger of God." Buddhists often consider Jesus a reincarnation of Buddha. Any way you look at Jesus, his story is EPIC.

Unfortunately, many people try to read about him and come away with an epic fail. Maybe at some point in the past you decided to pick up a copy of The Bible and read about Jesus. Like many, you may not have read very far before finding the experience laborious and anything but entertaining or relaxing. There are a number of explanations for this, and they all motivated me to create *Epic*.

You may know that four men wrote four hard-to-categorize works. We call them Gospels. I describe them as mini-biographies that focus on the birth and last three years of Jesus' life. Matthew, Mark, and Luke are similar in style and tell similar stories, yet they do not have the order of events as a main goal. They group stories according to theme or emphasis. John is the fourth Gospel and the most different. However, all four include the arrest, crucifixion, and resurrection of Jesus. And this is done from four different perspectives, including different details, as would happen if any four storytellers recounted the same events. It all becomes a bit confusing to try to put together in a cohesive picture of the life of Jesus. So I spent seven-and-a-half years and 5000 hours doing it for you. What you are holding is a very careful harmonizing or synthesizing of these four authors' gospels into one epic narrative. While we cannot be dogmatic about the order of events, there is enough detail given to create a viable chronology for Jesus' life. (You can learn more about that at the website bradandjayme.com.)

In addition to the four perspectives, the columns, verse and chapter numbers, and the myriad of notes in Bibles further complicate reading the life of Jesus. While this makes for good study, it makes for poor reading. Then, everything is compounded by the sentence structure produced in English translations from Greek, which is different from modern English sentence structure. Therefore, I purposed to create a new translation that bends syntax (sentence structure) far enough to be easily read in modern English. The reading flow achieved does not sacrifice anything in communication or truth. I left nothing out from the four Gospels, and I have added nothing more than transitional words for ease of reading.

The new translation is supported by formatting expected in any good novel. The footnotes indicate where the following stories can be found in any Bible. At the back, you will find a table of the travels, stories, and teachings of Jesus referenced through the four gospels.

If you purchased the electronic version you have the color version followed by the black and white *Epic* (such a deal!). The color version features a distinct color assigned to each author. Matthew/Blue, Mark/Orange, Luke/Green, John/Purple. Black signifies that two or more authors said the same thing. In this way, you are able to distinguish what each author uniquely contributes to each story.

So here's hoping you enjoy reading *Epic* – about the man many have argued to be the most influential person to ever live. Then you can answer the question posed throughout the stories about this carpenter:

"Who is this man?"

Chapters

In the Beginning

[1]In the beginning was the Word,
and the Word was with God,
and the Word was God.
He was in the beginning with God.
He made everything;
not a single thing was made without him.
Life was in him,
and the life was the light of men.
The light shines in the darkness;
the darkness could not comprehend or conquer it.

God sent a man named John as a witness to the light so that everyone could believe through him. He was not the light, just someone sent to tell what he saw about the light.

The true light was coming into the world, and it would shine on everyone, but even though he was in the world he made, it did not understand him. He came to his own people and they wouldn't accept him. However, he empowered everyone who accepted him and believed in his name to become the children of God. These people were not born by blood or the flesh's will or man's will. Instead, God gave birth to them.

The Word became a physical being and lived among us, and we looked at his glory. It was the glory of the Father's only son – full of grace and truth.

John told what he saw, even shouting, "This is the one I told you about when I said, 'He who comes after me is greater than I am because he was before me!'"

---

[1]John 1:1-18

Everything we have, we got from his fullness – grace upon grace upon grace. While Moses gave us the Law, Jesus Christ brought us grace and truth.

No one has ever seen God. But the one and only God, who was born out of the Father, came and revealed Him to us.

Miraculous Births

[2]Many have decided to write the stories that were handed down to us by the people who actually saw it all happen from the beginning. Those people became servants of the word. Therefore, I thought writing an orderly account of all that happened around us would be a good idea. So I went back and carefully investigated all the stories from their beginning in order that you, most excellent Theophilus, would be able to know how sure are those things you have been taught.

[3]Now this is the beginning of the gospel of Jesus Christ, the Son of God.

[4]While Herod was the king of Judea, there was a certain priest named Zacharias. He was part of the priestly line of Abijah, and his wife Elisabeth was a descendent of Aaron. God regarded both of them as righteous since they walked blamelessly in all his rules and commandments. Yet they had no child because Elisabeth was barren and now they were both rather old.

One day when it was his division's turn and the priestly custom, Zacharias served as the priest before God. He was chosen by lot to go into the Lord's temple and burn incense.

During that time, a whole crowd was praying outside the temple as an angel of the Lord appeared to Zacharias standing on the right side of the altar of incense. When he saw the angel, he was disturbed and gripped with fear.

"Don't be afraid Zacharias," said the angel. "Your prayer was heard; your wife Elisabeth will have a boy. Name him John. You will be so happy and full of joy, and many will rejoice when he is born because he will be great in the Lord's sight. He must not drink wine or liquor, but he will be filled

---

[2]Luke 1:1-4
[3]Mark 1:1
[4]Luke 1:5-25

with the Holy Spirit even while in his mother's womb. In time, he will turn many of the children of Israel to the Lord their God. He will also go before him in the spirit and power of Elijah to turn the hearts of the fathers to the children and the disobedient to the wisdom of the just. All this will get the people ready for the Lord."

"How can I be sure?" Zacharias replied. "I am an old man now, and my wife is old as well."

"I am Gabriel. I stand in the presence of God, and I was sent to speak to you and to tell you this good news. Since you didn't believe me, you won't be able to speak until all these things happen on time."

Meanwhile, the people waited for Zacharias and wondered why he was staying in the temple for so long. When he came out, he couldn't speak. He just kept making signs to them, and they realized that he had seen a vision in the temple.

Finally, his days of ministry were done and he went home. After some time, Elisabeth conceived and lived in private for five months saying, "The Lord saw me, and this is how he decided to work things out so others could see that my disgrace is gone."

[5]In Elisabeth's sixth month, God sent the angel Gabriel to the Galilean city of Nazareth to a virgin named Mary who was engaged to a man named Joseph, a descendant of David.

The angel came to her and said, "Hello favored one, the Lord is with you. You are blessed among women!"

As Mary looked at Gabriel, she was disturbed and wondered what this greeting meant.

"Don't be afraid Mary, for you have found favor with God, and you will conceive and give birth to a son and name him Jesus. He will be great, and he will be called the Son of the Most High. Then the Lord God will give him the throne

---

[5]Matt 1:18-2:23; Luke 1:26-2:52

of his father David, and he will reign over the house of Jacob forever. His kingdom will never end."

"How can this happen since I am a virgin?" Mary wondered.

"The Holy Spirit will come over you and overshadow you with the power of the Most High. Therefore, that holy thing you will give birth to shall be called the Son of God. Even your cousin Elisabeth, whom they call barren, has conceived a son in her old age, and she's six months along. Nothing will be impossible with God."

"I am the Lord's servant," said Mary. "Let it happen to me just like you say."

Then the angel left.

During those days, Mary got up and hurried to a town of Judah in the hill country. Arriving at Zacharias' house, she went in and greeted Elisabeth, and as Elisabeth heard the greeting, the baby jumped in her womb. She was filled with the Holy Spirit as she exclaimed, "Blessed are you among women, and blessed is the fruit of your womb. What brings the mother of my Lord to visit me? Listen! When I heard the sound of your Hello, the baby jumped inside me for joy. She is greatly blessed for believing because the things the Lord told her will happen!"

And Mary sang,
"My soul magnifies the Lord,
and my spirit rejoices in God my Savior.
For he looked on the
humble state of his servant girl,
and from now on all generations
will call me blessed
because the Mighty One
has done great things for me
and holy is his name.
His mercy is on those who fear him
from generation to generation.
He has shown strength with his arm;
he has scattered the proud

in the imagination of their hearts.
He has knocked the mighty from their thrones
and exalted those who were humble.
He has filled the hungry with good things
and sent the rich away empty.
He helped his servant Israel
as He remembered his mercy;
Just as he spoke to our fathers –
to Abraham and to his descendants forever."

So Mary stayed with Elisabeth about three months before going home.

Now the birth of Jesus Christ happened like this: When his mother Mary was engaged to Joseph, before they came together, she was found to be pregnant by the Holy Spirit.

Her husband Joseph was an honorable man and refused to shame her publicly. Instead, he decided to end their engagement secretly, but as he thought about it, the angel of the Lord appeared to him in a dream saying, "Joseph, son of David, don't be afraid to take Mary as your wife. The Holy Spirit is the one who made her conceive. She will give birth to a son, and you will name him Jesus because he will save his people from their sins."

All this was done so that it would happen just as the Lord spoke through the prophet saying, *[6]Behold, a virgin will be pregnant and will give birth to a son, and they will name him Emmanuel, which means, God with us.*

Joseph woke up and did as the angel of the Lord had told him and took Mary as his wife. But he had no relations with her until after she had given birth to her firstborn son, and he named him Jesus.

Now the time came for Elisabeth to deliver and she gave birth to a son. Her neighbors and cousins rejoiced with her as they heard how the Lord had shown her such mercy.

---

[6] Isaiah 7:14; 9:6,7; 8:10

On the eighth day, when they came to circumcise the child, they called him Zacharias after the name of his father, but his mother said, "No, his name is John."

"None of your family is called by this name," they replied.

And they made signs to his father asking him what the baby's name should be. He asked for a tablet and wrote, "His name is John."

They all marveled. Immediately his mouth was opened, his tongue was set free, and he spoke and praised God.

Everyone who lived around there became afraid, and all these things were talked about throughout the hill country of Judea as everyone who heard it kept it close to heart saying, "What a child this will be!" So the hand of the Lord was with him.

Then his father Zacharias was filled with the Holy Spirit and prophesied:

"Blessed be the Lord God of Israel,
for he has visited and redeemed his people
and has raised up a horn of salvation for us
in the house of his servant David,
just as he told us by the mouth
of his holy prophets from long ago
that we should be saved from our enemies
and from the hand of all who hate us
to perform the mercy promised to our fathers
and to remember his holy covenant –
the oath which he promised to our father Abraham
that he would grant to us
that we being delivered out of the hand of our enemies
might serve him without fear
in holiness and righteousness before him
all the days of our life.
And you child,
will be called the prophet of the Most High,
for you will go before the face of the Lord
to prepare his ways

and to give the knowledge of salvation to his people
by the remission of their sins
through the tender mercy of our God,
whereby the Dayspring from on high has visited us
to give light to those who sit in darkness
and the shadow of death
to guide our feet into the way of peace."

And the child grew and became strong in spirit and was in the deserts until the day he appeared publicly to Israel.

Then it happened in those days that a decree went out from Caesar Augustus that all the world should be taxed. (This census first occurred when Cyrenius was governor of Syria.) Everyone went to his own city to pay taxes, including Joseph and his pregnant fiancée, Mary.

Since Joseph was a descendant of David, he took Mary and left the Galilean city of Nazareth to go to the Judean city of Bethlehem, also called the city of David.

While there, the time came for her to deliver, and she gave birth to her firstborn son and wrapped him in cloths and laid him in a manger because there were no rooms left in the inn.

Not far away that night, shepherds were in the fields watching over their flock, and an angel of the Lord appeared to them as the glory of the Lord lit up all around them, and they were very afraid. "Don't be afraid," said the angel. "I have good news of a great joy and it is for all people. On this day, in the city of David, a Savior is born to you. He is Lord Messiah, and the sign for you is this: you will find a baby wrapped in cloths and lying in a manger."

Suddenly, a great number of heavenly beings were with the angel praising God and saying, "Glory to God in the highest and peace on Earth! This is for everyone with whom he is pleased!"

When the angels went back to Heaven, the shepherds said, "Let's go to Bethlehem and see what the Lord is telling us has happened."

So they hurried and found Mary and Joseph and the baby who was lying in the manger. When they saw it all, the shepherds declared to them what they had been told about this child. Everyone who heard it marveled at what the shepherds revealed to them. As for Mary, she treasured these things, pondering them in her heart. Soon the shepherds went back glorifying and praising God for everything they had heard and seen, just as they were told.

At the end of eight days, when he was circumcised, the child was called Jesus, the name the angel gave him before he was conceived.

Then the time came for their purification according to the Law of Moses, so they brought Jesus up to Jerusalem to present him to the Lord. It is written in the Law of the Lord: [7]*Every male who first opens the womb shall be called holy to the Lord.* They also had to offer a sacrifice that is commanded in the Law of the Lord – [8]*a pair of turtledoves or two young pigeons.*

At this time there was a man in Jerusalem named Simeon; he was righteous and devout, waiting for the consolation of Israel. The Holy Spirit was on him and had revealed to him that he would not die before he had seen the Lord's Messiah. He came in the Spirit to the temple, and when the parents brought in the child Jesus to fulfill the customs of the Law, he picked Jesus up in his arms and blessed God saying, "Lord, now you are letting your servant leave in peace, just like you said you would. My eyes have seen the salvation that you have prepared in the presence of all peoples – [9]*a light for revelation to the Gentiles and glory to your people Israel.*"

His father and his mother marveled at what was said about him. Then Simeon blessed them and said to Mary, his mother, "Behold, this child is appointed for the rise and fall

---

[7] Exodus 13:2,12; Numbers 3:13; 8:17
[8] Leviticus 5:11; 12:
[9] Psalms 119:166,174; Isaiah 52:10

of many in Israel and for a sign that will be opposed. Mary, a sword will pierce through your own soul as well, and thoughts from many hearts will be revealed."

Also at the temple was a prophetess from Asher's tribe named Anna, who was Phanuel's daughter. She was quite old and had lived with her husband for seven years after being married. Then she was a widow until age eighty-four. She never left the temple. Instead, she served God night and day by fasting and praying. She came in right away thanking the Lord and telling everyone waiting for the redemption of Israel about Jesus.

Now after Jesus was born in Bethlehem of Judea during King Herod's time, surprisingly, wise men from the east arrived in Jerusalem saying, "Where is he? The one born to be the King of the Jews? We have seen his star in the east and have come to worship him."

When King Herod heard these things, he was troubled and all Jerusalem with him. He gathered all the chief priests and scribes of the people together and demanded to know from them where the Messiah was to be born, and they told him, "In Bethlehem of Judea, as it is written by the prophet:

[10]*And you Bethlehem, in the land of Judah, are not the least among the princes of Judah, for out of you will come a ruler who will shepherd my people Israel.*

Then Herod met with the wise men secretly and learned exactly what time the star appeared. He sent them to Bethlehem, telling them, "Go and search carefully for the young child, and when you have found him, tell me so I can come and worship him also."

After hearing the king, they set out, and remarkably the star they saw in the east went before them until it came and stood over where the child was. When they saw the star, they rejoiced, entered the house, and saw the child with Mary his mother. Falling down, they worshiped him. When they had

---

[10] Micah 5:2

opened their treasures, they gave him gifts of gold, frankincense, and myrrh.

Later, God warned them in a dream that they should not return to Herod, so they left and took another route to their own country. After they left, an angel of the Lord appeared to Joseph in a dream, saying, "Get up, take the child and his mother and flee into Egypt. Stay there until I tell you because Herod will search for the child to kill him."

He got up, took the child and his mother by night and went to Egypt. He remained there until Herod died so that what was spoken by the Lord through the prophet might be fulfilled: [11]*I called my son out of Egypt.*"

Herod was enraged when he realized he'd been tricked by the wise men. He calculated the time he learned from them and then killed all the children, two years old and under, who were in Bethlehem and the surrounding coasts. Then what Jeremiah the prophet said was fulfilled: [12]*A voice was heard weeping and mourning in Ramah. It's Rachel weeping for her children, and she would not be comforted because they are no more.*

After Herod died, the child and his parents were still in Egypt, and they had performed everything according to the Law of the Lord. An angel of the Lord also appeared in a dream to Joseph saying, "Get up, take the child and his mother and go to the land of Israel, for those who wanted to kill the child are dead." He got up and they came into Israel. But when he heard that Archelaus was reigning in Judea in the place of his father Herod, he was afraid to go there (along with being warned by God in a dream) so he went to live in the Galilean city of Nazareth. This would also fulfill what was spoken by the prophets: [13]*He shall be called a Nazarene.* While there, Jesus grew and became strong and filled with wisdom. God's favor was on him.

---

[11] Hosea 11:1
[12] Jeremiah 31:15
[13] Not recorded in OT

Every year, his parents went to Jerusalem at the feast of the Passover. One year when he was twelve years old, they visited, and afterward they were returning home. But unknown to Joseph and his mother, the boy Jesus stayed behind in Jerusalem. Assuming he was with the group, they traveled a day's journey and then looked for him among their relatives and acquaintances. They didn't find him, so they returned to look for him in Jerusalem.

They found him three days later in the temple, sitting among the teachers, listening to them and asking them questions. Everyone who heard him was astonished at his answers and his understanding.

When they saw him, they were amazed, and his mother said, "Son, why have you treated us this way? Your father and I have been searching for you and grieving."

"Why were you looking for me?" Jesus asked. "Didn't you know that I have to be about my Father's business?"

They didn't understand what he was talking about. Still, he went down with them to Nazareth and submitted himself to them while his mother kept these sayings in her heart. All along, Jesus continued to grow in wisdom and in stature and in favor with God and man.

The Early Days

[14]In the fifteenth year of the reign of Tiberius Caesar, Pontius Pilate was governor of Judea, Herod was tetrarch of Galilee, his brother Philip was tetrarch of the region of Ituraea and Trachonitis, and Lysanias was tetrarch of Abilene. It was also during the high priesthood of Annas and Caiaphas that the word of God came to John, the son of Zechariah, in the wilderness. Then John, "the Baptizer," went into the entire region around the Jordan preaching a baptism of repentance for the forgiveness of sins. That's the word written in the book of Isaiah the prophet:

[15]*Behold, I send my messenger before your face*
who will prepare your way –
The voice of one crying in the wilderness –
prepare the way of the Lord,
make his paths straight.
Every valley will be filled
and every mountain and hill flattened,
and the crooked will be made straight,
and the rough places will become smooth roads,
and all mankind will see the salvation of God.

The people from the regions of Judea, Jerusalem, and around the Jordan were going out and being immersed by John in the Jordan River as they confessed their sins.

John wore clothes of camel's hair with a leather belt around his waist, and he ate locusts and wild honey. He preached, saying, "You must change your life because the kingdom of Heaven is here."

He also said to the crowds, including the Pharisees and Sadducees coming to be immersed by him, "You generation of snakes! Who warned you to run from the wrath to come?

---

[14]Mark 1:2-8; Matthew 3:1-12; Luke 3:1-18
[15] Malachi 3:1; Isaiah 40:3-4

If you are repenting, bear the fruit of it, and don't think about saying to yourselves, 'Abraham is our father.' For I tell you, God is able to raise up children for Abraham from these rocks. Right now the axe is laid on the root of the trees. Therefore, every tree that does not bear good fruit is cut down and thrown into the fire."

"So what should we do?" the crowds asked.

"Whoever has two coats should give one to the person who doesn't have one, and whoever has food should do the same."

Tax collectors also came to be immersed, saying, "Teacher, what should we do?"

"Don't collect more than you're supposed to."

"What about us, what should we do?" asked the soldiers.

"Don't extort money from anyone by threats or false accusations. Also, be content with your wages."

Expectations and questions filled the people's hearts concerning John. They wondered whether he could be the Messiah. John told them all, "I immerse you with water for repentance, but the one who is mightier than I am is coming. I'm not worthy to kneel down and untie his sandals or carry them! I have immersed you in water, but he will immerse you with the Holy Spirit and with fire. His winnowing fork is in his hand, and he will clear his threshing floor and gather the wheat into his barn, but the chaff he will burn with unquenchable fire." With these and many other words John exhorted the people and preached the good news to them.

[16]In those days, Jesus came from Nazareth in Galilee to the Jordan. He came to be immersed by John, but John tried to stop him, saying, "I need to be immersed by you. Why are you coming to me?"

"You must let it be this way," Jesus answered. "This is how we fulfill all that is righteous." Then John gave in. He immersed all the people and also Jesus. And as soon as Jesus

---

[16]Mark 1:9-11; Matthew 3:13-17; Luke 3:21-22

went up from the water, the Heavens were torn open to him, and he saw the Spirit of God coming down in bodily form like a dove. It came to rest on him, and remarkably, a voice from Heaven said, "This is my beloved Son; I am so pleased with him."

[17]Full of the Holy Spirit, Jesus immediately returned from the Jordan. And the Spirit led him into the wilderness among the wild animals to be tempted by the Devil.

He ate nothing during that time, and after fasting forty days and forty nights, he was hungry. Then the Devil (the tempter) came and said to him, "If you are the Son of God, command these rocks to become loaves of bread."

But he answered, "It is written: [18]*A man won't live on bread alone, but by every word that comes from God's mouth.*"

The Devil also took him to the holy city Jerusalem and set him on the pinnacle of the temple and said to him, "If you are the Son of God, throw yourself down, for it is written: [19]*He will command his angels to guard you,* and *On their hands they will carry you so that you won't trip over a rock.*"

"Again, it is written," said Jesus, [20]"*You shall not put the Lord your God to the test.*"

Then the Devil took him to a very high mountain, and in a moment of time showed him all the kingdoms of the world and their glory, saying, "I will give you power over all this and their glory, for it has been delivered to me, and I can give it to anyone I choose. It will all be yours if you worship me."

"Leave, Satan!" demanded Jesus. "For it is written: [21]*You will worship the Lord your God and serve only him.*"

---

[17]Mark 1:12-13; Matthew 4:1-11; Luke 4:1-13
[18] Deuteronomy 8:3
[19] Psalm 91:11,12
[20] Deuteronomy 6:16
[21] Deuteronomy 6:13, 10:20

And when the Devil had finished every temptation, he left him to wait for a better time. Then angels came to help Jesus.

+ + +

[22]This is John's testimony when the Jews sent priests and Levites from Jerusalem to Bethany across the Jordan where John was immersing. They were asking him, "Who are you?"

He confessed, "I am not the Messiah."

"What then? Are you Elijah?"

"I am not."

"Are you the Prophet?"

"No."

"Who are you? We need to give an answer to those who sent us. Say something about yourself."

"I am the *voice of one crying out in the wilderness;* [23]*Make the way of the Lord straight,*' just as the prophet Isaiah said."

These men had been sent from the Pharisees so they asked him, "Why are you immersing if you are neither the Messiah, nor Elijah, nor the Prophet?"

"I immerse with water," said John, "but among you stands someone you don't know. He comes after me and I am not worthy to untie his sandal."

The next day he saw Jesus coming toward him and said, "See! The Lamb of God who takes away the sin of the world! This is the one I'm talking about when I say, 'After me comes a man who is over me because he was before me.' I did not know him, but this is why I came immersing with water so that he might be revealed to Israel."

John continued his witness saying, "I saw the Spirit descend from Heaven like a dove, and it remained on him. I did not know him, but he who sent me to immerse with

---

[22]John 1:19-51

[23] Isaiah 40:3

water said to me, 'The one you see the Spirit come down and stay on, this is the one who immerses with the Holy Spirit.' I've seen and testified that this is the Son of God."

The next day, John was standing again with two of his disciples, and he looked at Jesus walking by and said, "Look! The Lamb of God!"

The two disciples heard him say this so they followed Jesus. Jesus turned and saw them following and asked, "What are you looking for?"

"Rabbi, where are you staying?" they asked. (Rabbi means teacher.)

"Come with me and you'll see."

They came and saw where he was staying and remained with him that day because it was about 4:00 p.m. One of the two who heard John speak and followed Jesus was Andrew, Simon Peter's brother. First, he found his own brother Simon and said to him, "We have found the Messiah!" (Messiah means the anointed one.)

Andrew brought Simon. Jesus looked at him and said, "You are Simon, John's son. You will be called Cephas." (Cephas means rock.)

The next day, Jesus decided to go to Galilee. He found Philip and said, "Follow me."

Philip was from Bethsaida, the city of Andrew and Peter. Then Philip found Nathanael and said, "We've found him! The one Moses in the Law and also the prophets wrote about – it's Jesus of Nazareth – Joseph's son!"

"Can anything good come out of Nazareth?" Nathanael asked.

"You'll have to come and see," said Philip.

When Jesus saw Nathanael coming toward him, he said, "Look, a true Israelite – there is no deception in him!"

"How do you know me?" wondered Nathanael.

"Before Philip called you, I saw you under the fig tree."

"Rabbi, you are the Son of God!" declared Nathanael. "You are the King of Israel!"

"You believe because I said, 'I saw you under the fig tree'? You're going to see greater things than these," said Jesus. "The truth is – you will see Heaven opened and God's angels ascending and descending on the Son of Man."

[24]On the third day there was a wedding at Cana in Galilee, and Jesus' mother was there. Jesus was also invited to the wedding with his disciples. When the wine ran out, his mother said to him, "There's no more wine."

"Woman, what does that have to do with me?" Jesus asked. "It's not time for me yet."

"Do whatever he tells you," his mother said to the servants.

There were six stone water pots nearby for the Jewish custom of cleansing, each holding twenty or thirty gallons. Jesus said to the servants, "Fill the jars with water."

They filled them up to the top accordingly, and he said to them, "Now draw some out and take it to the master of ceremony."

They took some and the master of ceremony tasted the water that had become wine, but he didn't know where it came from – only the servants who had drawn the water knew that. The master of ceremony called the bridegroom and said to him, "Everyone serves the good wine first, and when people have become merry, they serve the cheaper wine, but you kept the good wine until now."

Jesus performed his first sign there at Cana in Galilee, making his glory visible, and his disciples believed in him.

After this he went with his mother, his brothers, and his disciples down to Capernaum where they stayed for a few days.

[25]When it was nearly time for the Passover of the Jews, Jesus went up to Jerusalem. He found people in the temple selling oxen, sheep, and pigeons. He also found money-

---

[24]John 2:1-12
[25]John 2:13-25

changers sitting there, so he made a whip and drove them all out of the temple with the sheep and oxen. He poured out the coins of the bankers and overturned their tables, telling the pigeon salesmen, "Get this out of here! Do not make my Father's house a business center!"

His disciples remembered that it was written: [26]*Zeal for your house consumes me.*

So the Jews demanded, "What sign do you show us that gives you the right to do these things?"

"Tear down this temple, and in three days I will raise it back up," said Jesus.

"It has taken forty-six years to build this temple," they replied, "and you can raise it up in three days?"

But he was talking about the temple of his body. After he was raised from the dead, his disciples remembered that he had said this and believed the Scripture and the word that Jesus had spoken.

While he was in Jerusalem at the Passover Feast, many people believed in his name as they saw the miracles he was doing. However, Jesus didn't entrust himself to them because he knew all people and didn't need them to bear witness about him – especially since he knew people, inside and out.

+ + +

[27]There was a Jewish ruler named Nicodemus. He was a Pharisee who came to Jesus at night and said to him, "Rabbi, we know you come from God as a teacher because no one can do the miracles you do unless God is with him."

Jesus said, "The truth is – unless a person is born again he cannot see the Kingdom of God."

---

[26] Psalms 69:9
[27] John 3:1-4:2

"How can a man be born when he is old?" Nicodemus asked. "Can he climb into his mother's womb and be born a second time?"

"The truth is – unless a person is born of water and the Spirit, he cannot enter the kingdom of God. Whatever is born of the flesh is flesh, and whatever is born of the Spirit is spirit. Don't marvel that I said to you, 'You must be born again.' The wind blows where it wishes, and you hear its sound, but you don't know where it comes from or where it's going. It's the same way with everyone who is born of the Spirit."

"How can it be this way?" Nicodemus asked.

"Are you the teacher of Israel but you don't understand these things? I speak the truth when I tell you, we speak of what we know and witness to what we've seen, but you don't accept our testimony. If you don't believe when I tell you about earthly things, how can you believe if I tell you heavenly things? No one has gone up into Heaven except the one who came down from Heaven – the Son of Man. Just as Moses lifted up the snake in the wilderness, so the Son of Man has to be lifted up that whoever believes in him will have the life of the age to come."

"God loved the world so much that he gave his only Son so that whoever puts their faith in him would not be lost or perish, but have life for the ages. God did not send his Son into the world to condemn the world, but that the world might be saved through him. Whoever puts faith in him is not condemned, but whoever does not believe is condemned already because he has not believed in the name of God's only son. Here is the judgment: the light has come into the world, and people loved the darkness instead of the light because their actions were evil. Everyone who does wicked things hates the light. They don't come to the light because they don't want their actions exposed. In contrast, whoever does what is true comes to the light, that way it can be obvious that their works have been carried out in God."

Later, Jesus and his disciples went into the Judean countryside, and he stayed with them and was immersing. John was also immersing at Aenon near Salim because there was plenty of water there, and people were coming and being immersed. (John had not been put in prison at this time.)

A disagreement arose between some of John's disciples and a Jew over purification. They came to John and said to him, "Rabbi, the one who was with you across the Jordan, the one you witnessed about – look at him! He's immersing and all the people are going to him."

John answered, "A person cannot receive anything unless it is given to him from Heaven. You yourselves witnessed me saying, 'I am not Messiah, but I have been sent ahead of him.' The bridegroom has the bride. The bridegroom's friend stands and hears him and rejoices greatly at the bridegroom's voice. Now my joy is complete. He must increase, and I must decrease."

The one who comes from above is above all. The one who is of the earth belongs to the earth, and so he speaks in an earthly manner. The one who comes from Heaven is above all. He witnesses to what he has seen and heard, but no one accepts his testimony. Whoever receives his testimony certifies this – that God is true. The one God sent speaks God's words, for he gives the Spirit without measure. The Father loves the Son and has given all things into his hand. Whoever believes in the Son has life for the ages. Whoever does not obey the Son will not see life. Instead, God's wrath will remain on him.

The Pharisees also had heard that Jesus was making and immersing more disciples than John, although Jesus didn't immerse anyone, his disciples were the ones doing the immersing.

[28]Then Herod the tetrarch, who had been rebuked by John concerning Herodias, his brother's wife, and for all the

---

[28]Mark 1:14; Luke 3:19-20

evil things that Herod had done, added this to it all – he put John in prison.

[29]When Jesus heard these things, he left Judea and headed into Galilee. He had to go through Samaria and he came to a Samaritan town called Sychar, near the field that Jacob had given to his son Joseph. Jacob's well was there, and Jesus, tired from the trip, was sitting beside the well. It was about the sixth hour.

A Samaritan woman came to draw water while his disciples had gone into the city to buy food. Jesus said to her, "Give me a drink."

Since Jews didn't have dealings with Samaritans, she replied, "How can you ask me for a drink? You're a Jew and I'm a Samaritan woman!"

"If you knew God's gift and who it is that's saying to you, 'Give me a drink,' you would have asked him, and he would have given you living water," Jesus replied.

"Sir, you have nothing to draw water with, and the well is deep. Where do you get that living water? Are you greater than our father Jacob? He gave us the well and he drank from it himself, along with his sons and his livestock."

"Everyone who drinks this water will get thirsty again," he said. "But whoever drinks the water I will give him will never be thirsty. The water I will give him will become a spring of water welling up in him to whole life."

"Sir, give me this water so I will not be thirsty or have to come here to draw it."

"Go call your husband and come here."

"I don't have a husband."

"Well said, 'I don't have a husband,' even though you've had five husbands, and the man you're with now is not your husband. You're telling the truth."

---

[29]Matthew 4:12; John 4:3-43

"Sir, I can tell that you are a prophet. Our fathers worshiped on this mountain, but you say that people ought to go to Jerusalem to worship."

"Woman, believe me, the time is coming when neither on this mountain nor in Jerusalem will you worship the Father. You worship what you do not know; we worship what we know, for salvation is from the Jews. But the hour is coming, and is now here, when the true worshipers will worship the Father in spirit and truth. These are the people the Father is seeking to worship him. God is spirit, and those who worship him must worship in spirit and truth."

"I know that Messiah is coming." (She was referring to the one called Messiah.) "When he comes, he will tell us everything."

"That would be me, the one talking to you," Jesus replied.

Soon his disciples returned and were amazed that he was talking with a woman, but no one said, "What do you want?" or "Why are you talking with her?"

Then the woman left her water jar, went into town and announced to the people, "Come with me and see a man who told me everything I have ever done. Can this be Messiah?" So the people came from town to see him.

Meanwhile, the disciples urged him, saying, "Rabbi, eat something."

"I have food to eat that you don't know about," he said.

"Has anyone brought him something to eat?" the disciples were asking one another.

"My food is to do the will of him who sent me and to accomplish his work," Jesus told them. "Don't you say, 'There are four months, then comes the harvest?' I tell you to open your eyes and see that the fields are white for harvest. The one who reaps is already receiving his pay and gathering fruit for the life of the ages, that sower and reaper may rejoice together. The old saying is true, 'One sows and another reaps.' I sent you to reap what you didn't work for. Others have labored as well, and you have entered into their work."

As a result, many Samaritans from that town believed in him because of the woman's testimony, "He told me all that I ever did."

So when the Samaritans came to him, they asked him to stay with them, and he stayed there two days. Then many more believed because of his word. They said to the woman, "We no longer believe because of what you said. Instead, we have heard for ourselves, and we know for sure that this is the Savior of the world."

Home in Capernaum, Life in Galilee

[30]After those two days, Jesus returned in the power of the Spirit to Galilee declaring, "The time is fulfilled and the kingdom of God is near. Repent and believe the good news!" This is the gospel of God that Jesus came into Galilee proclaiming. After visiting Nazareth, where he concluded that a prophet has no honor in his own hometown, he went to live in Capernaum by the sea in the territory of Zebulun and Naphtali. This fulfilled what was said through the prophet Isaiah:

> [31]*The land of Zebulun and the land of Naphtali toward the sea, beyond the Jordan, Galilee of the Gentiles – the people who sat in darkness saw a great light, and the people who sat in the region and shadow of death – the dawn has come!*

Then he came again to Cana in Galilee where he had turned water into wine. Hearing that Jesus had come from Judea to Galilee, an official from Capernaum went to him and begged him to come and heal his son who was near death.

Jesus said to him, "Unless you see signs and wonders, you just won't believe."

"Sir, come or my child will die," he pleaded.

"Go. Your son will live," Jesus assured him.

The man went home believing what Jesus said, and along the way, his servants met him saying, "Your son is alive!"

"What time did he begin to get better?"

"The fever left him yesterday at the seventh hour," they replied.

The father realized it was at the same time that Jesus said, "Your son will live." So he believed along with his whole

---

[30]Mark 1:14-15; Matthew 4:13-17; Luke 4:14a
John 4:43, 44, 46-54
[31] Isaiah 9:1; 60:1-3

household. This was Jesus' second sign after coming from Judea to Galilee.

[32]The Galileans who had gone to the feast in Jerusalem and witnessed all that he had done there, welcomed him. At the same time, his fame spread through all the surrounding country. He also taught in their synagogues, and everyone thought very highly of him.

One day while walking by the Sea of Galilee, he saw two brothers, Simon (also called Peter) and Andrew his brother, casting a net into the sea because they were fishermen. Jesus called to them, "Follow me, and I will make you fishers of men."

Right away, they left their nets and followed him. Going on from there, he saw two other brothers, James and John, in the boat with their father Zebedee, mending their nets. Immediately he called them, and they left their father Zebedee in the boat with the hired servants and followed him.

[33]Later, they went down to the Galilean City of Capernaum. On the Sabbath, he went to the synagogue and was teaching, and they were astonished because he taught them with authority, but not like the scribes because his word possessed power.

In the synagogue there was a man with an unclean spirit – a demon. He cried out with a loud voice, "AAAHHH! WHAT ARE YOU GOING TO DO WITH US, JESUS OF NAZARETH? ARE YOU GOING TO DESTROY US? I KNOW WHO YOU ARE – THE HOLY ONE OF GOD." The demon threw the man down in the middle of them all.

"Be quiet, and come out of him!" Jesus demanded as the demons were convulsing the man and screaming loudly. Then it came out of him, and the man was unharmed.

---

[32]Mark 1:16-20; Matthew 4:18-22; Luke 4:14b-15; John 4:45
[33]Mark 1:21-28; Luke 4:31-37

The people were all amazed and asked each other, "What is this word?"

"A new teaching with authority and power!" answered others. "He commands even the unclean spirits, and they obey him and come out!"

And more reports went out, spreading his fame everywhere around the region of Galilee.

[34]Then he left the synagogue and went to Simon Peter and Andrew's house, along with James and John.

At this time, Simon's mother-in-law was sick with a high fever, and they told Jesus about her. He came and stood over her, took her by the hand, and helped her up. Then he rebuked the fever and it left. She got up at once and started serving them.

That evening at sundown, they brought all who were sick with various diseases or oppressed by demons. The whole city was gathered at the door as Jesus laid his hands on every one of them. He healed them and cast demons out of many with a word. The demons would come out screaming, "YOU ARE THE SON OF GOD!" But he rebuked them and wouldn't allow the demons to speak because they knew he was the Messiah. This fulfilled what the prophet Isaiah said: [35]*He took our illnesses and bore our diseases.*

Very early the next morning, Jesus got up while it was still dark and went out to a desolate place to pray. Simon and the people who were with him searched for Jesus. They found him and said, "Everyone is looking for you."

They tried to keep him from leaving, but he said to them, "Let's go on to the next towns. I must preach the good news of the kingdom of God there also. I was sent for this purpose."

---

[34]Mark 1:29-39; Matthew 8:14-17; Luke 4:38-43
[35] Isaiah 53:4

[36]In one of the cities, a man full of leprosy came to him kneeling and falling on his face begging him, "Lord, if you want to, you can make me clean."

"I want to," Jesus said as he was moved with pity. Right then he stretched out his hand, touched him, and said, "Be clean."

Immediately, the leprosy was gone and he was made clean. Then Jesus spoke to him sternly, "Make sure that you don't tell anyone, but go show yourself to the priest and offer the gift that Moses commanded for your cleansing. That will be proof to them."

However, he went and spread the news, talking to everyone about it. It made such an impact that Jesus could no longer easily walk into a town. Instead, he withdrew to solitary places to pray. Still, large crowds were coming from all over to hear him and be healed of their infirmities.

So Jesus went throughout Galilee and Judea, teaching in their synagogues and proclaiming the gospel of the kingdom. He was healing every disease and affliction among the people. His fame spread through Syria, and they brought him all the sick, those afflicted with various diseases and pains, those oppressed by demons, epileptics, and paralytics. He healed them and cast out the demons. Large crowds were following him from Galilee, the Decapolis, Jerusalem, Judea, and beyond the Jordan.

[37]Some days later, Jesus returned to his own city of Capernaum, and it was reported that he was at home.

As he was teaching on one of those days, many people, along with Pharisees and teachers of the Law from every village of Galilee, Judea, and Jerusalem were sitting there, leaving no more room, not even at the door. He continued preaching the word to them and demonstrating the power of the Lord to heal.

---

[36]Mark 1:40-45; Matthew 4:23, 8:2-4; Luke 4:44,5:12-16
[37]Mark 2:1-12; Matthew 9:1-8; Luke 5:17-26

Remarkably, four men carried a paraplegic on a bed, trying to bring him in and lay him before Jesus, but they couldn't find a way to get him in because of the crowd. So they went up and removed the roof above him. They lowered him down on his bed through the tiles where Jesus was, in the middle of everyone. Jesus saw their faith and he said to the paraplegic, "Pick yourself up son. Your sins are forgiven."

With those words, the scribes and Pharisees began to question in their hearts, "How dare he talk like that? He is blaspheming! Who can forgive sins except God alone?"

Jesus knew their thoughts and unspoken questions in his spirit, and he asked them, "Why do you think evil in your hearts? Why do you question these things? Which is easier to say to the paraplegic, 'Your sins are forgiven' or 'Get up. Pick up your bed and walk?' But I want you to know that the Son of Man has authority on Earth to forgive sins." So he told the paraplegic, "Get up. Pick up your bed. And go home."

Immediately, he got up in front of them, picked up what he had been lying on and went home praising God! When the crowds saw it, they were scared and amazed that God had given such authority to men. They glorified God and were saying things like, "We never saw anything like this!" and "We have seen remarkable things today!"

[38]After this, he went again to the sea and taught the crowds that came to him. As he walked on, he saw tax collectors named Levi, the son of Alphaeus, and Matthew sitting at the tax booth, and he said to them, "Follow me."

They got up, left it all, and followed Jesus. Levi made a big feast for Jesus in his house, and as Jesus reclined at the table, many tax collectors and sinners were relaxing with him and his disciples because a lot of them followed him. When the Pharisees' scribes saw Jesus eating with them, they grumbled at his disciples, "Why do you and your teacher eat with tax collectors and sinners?"

---

[38] Mark 2:13-17; Matthew 9:9-13; Luke 5:27-32

"Healthy people don't need a doctor, only the sick do," Jesus said when he heard it. "Why don't you leave, but learn what this means, [39]*I desire mercy, and not sacrifice.* I have not come to call the righteous, but sinners to repentance."

[40] Sometime after this, there was a Jewish feast, and Jesus went up to Jerusalem. There is a pool by the Sheep Gate in Jerusalem called Bethesda (in Aramaic), which has five covered colonnades. Many people with all kinds of disabilities – blind, lame, paralyzed – were in the colonnades. One of them was a man who had been an invalid for thirty-eight years. Jesus saw him lying there and knew he had been sick for a long time. He asked, "Would you like to be healed?"

"Sir," the man answered, "I don't have anyone to put me into the pool when the water is stirred up, and while I am trying to get in, another steps in before me."

"Get up," said Jesus. "Pick up your bed and walk." Instantly, the man was healed. He picked up his bed and started walking.

It was a Sabbath day, and the Jews said to this man, "Today is the Sabbath; it's against the Law for you to pick up your bed."

"But the man who healed me told me, 'Pick up your bed and walk.'"

They demanded to know, "Who is this man who said you could, 'Pick up your bed and walk'?"

The man didn't know who had healed him, and Jesus had left when he saw the crowd gathering. Afterward, Jesus went and found him in the temple and said, "Look at you, you're well! If you don't want anything worse to happen to you, you shouldn't sin anymore."

Then the man went back and told the Jews that it was Jesus who had healed him. This was why the Jews were persecuting Jesus – he was doing these things on the Sabbath.

---

[39] Hosea 6:6
[40] John 5:1-47

Jesus answered them, "My Father is working now, and so am I."

This added another reason why the Jews were trying even harder to kill him – not only was he breaking the Sabbath, he was even calling God his own Father, making himself equal with God.

Jesus said, "The truth is – the Son can't make anything happen on his own; he only does what he sees the Father doing. Whatever the Father does, the Son does the same, and the Father shows the Son all that he's doing because he loves the son. He will show him even greater works than these. Then you can marvel; just as the Father raises the dead and gives them life, the Son also gives life to whomever he wants. The Father does not judge anyone. Instead, he has given all judgment to the Son, that everyone may honor the Son, just as they honor the Father. Whoever does not honor the Son does not honor the Father who sent him. The truth is – you will have the life of the coming age if you hear me and believe in the one who sent me. In that case, you won't come under judgment, but pass from death to life."

"I assure you, an hour is coming and is now here when the dead will hear the Son of God's voice, and the ones who do will live. Just as the Father has life in himself, he has also granted the Son to have life in himself, and he has given him authority to bring about judgment because he's the Son of Man. Don't let this surprise you since the time is coming when everyone in a grave will hear his voice and come out – those who have done good will experience the resurrection of life, and those who have done evil will go to the resurrection of judgment.

"I can't do anything on my own. I hear first, then I judge, and my judgment is just because I don't seek my own will but the will of him who sent me. You see, if I'm the only one who bears witness about me, then my testimony is not accepted as true.

Yet, there is another who bears witness about me, and I know that the testimony he bears about me is true. You sent to John, and he has borne witness to the truth. Not that the testimony I receive is from man, but I say these things so that you may be saved. He was a burning and shining lamp, and you were willing to rejoice for a while in his light. But the testimony I have is greater than that of John. For the works that the Father has given me to accomplish – the very works that I am doing – bear witness about me that the Father has sent me, and the Father who sent me has himself borne witness about me. You have never heard his voice or seen his form, and his word is not living in you because you do not believe the one whom he has sent. You search the Scriptures because you think you can get the life of the ages from them; they testify about me, yet you refuse to come to me that you may have life. I do not receive glory from people, and I know that you do not have the love of God within you. I have come in my Father's name, but you don't want me. If someone else comes in his own name, you'll receive him. Then again, how can you believe when you just trade glory with each other instead of seeking the glory that only God can give? And don't think that I will accuse you to the Father. Moses, the one you set your hope on, is the one who accuses you. If you believed Moses, you would believe me because he wrote about me. But if you don't believe what he wrote, how will you trust my words?"

+ + +

[41]One Sabbath, Jesus was going through the grain fields and his disciples were hungry. As they walked, they plucked grain, rubbed them in their hands and ate. When some of the Pharisees saw it, they said to him, "Look! Why are they doing what is not lawful on the Sabbath?"

"Have you never read what David did when he was in need and was hungry?" he asked them. "During the time of

---

[41]Mark 2:23-28, 3:1-8; Matthew 12:1-21; Luke 6:1-11

32

Abiathar the high priest, he and those who were with him entered God's house and ate the Bread of the Presence, which it is not lawful for any but the priests to eat. He also gave it to those with him. Or have you not read in the Law, how on the Sabbath, the priests in the temple break the Sabbath and yet have no guilt? I tell you there is something greater than the temple here. If you had known what this means, [42]*I desire mercy and not sacrifice*, you would not have condemned the innocent."

Then he added, "The Sabbath was made for man not man for the Sabbath. So the Son of Man is lord, even of the Sabbath."

On another Sabbath, he entered the synagogue and was teaching, and a man was there whose right hand was withered. They watched Jesus to see whether he would heal him on the Sabbath so that they might accuse him. They asked him, "Is it lawful to heal on the Sabbath?"

Jesus knew their thoughts and said to the man with the withered hand, "Come and stand here."

As he came and stood there, Jesus asked them, "Is it lawful on the Sabbath to do good or to do harm, to save life or to kill?"

They didn't make a sound. Jesus looked around at them with anger, grieved at the hardness of their hearts. He said, "Which one of you who has a sheep will not grab it and pull it out if it falls into a pit on the Sabbath? How much more valuable is a man than a sheep? So it is lawful to do good on the Sabbath."

Then, after looking around at all of them, he told the man, "Stretch out your hand." He stretched it out, and his hand was restored, healthy like the other.

The Pharisees were infuriated. They went out at once and met with the Herodians, conspiring together how to destroy Jesus.

---

[42] Hosea 6:6

Aware of this, Jesus withdrew from there with his disciples to the sea, and a great crowd followed from Galilee, Judea, Jerusalem, Idumea, Tyre, Sidon, and from beyond the Jordan. When they heard all that he was doing, they came to him and he healed them all and ordered them not to make him known. This was to fulfill what was spoken by the prophet Isaiah:

[43]Behold, my servant – the one I chose,
my beloved – the one who pleases me.
I will put my Spirit on him,
and he will proclaim justice to the Gentiles.
He will not argue or cry aloud
nor will anyone hear his voice in the streets.
A bruised reed he will not break,
and a smoldering wick he will not be extinguished
until he brings justice to victory,
and in his name the Gentiles will hope.

+ + +

[44]On another day, he was standing by the lake of Gennesaret, while the crowd was pressing in on him to hear the word of God. He had told his disciples to have a boat ready so the crowd wouldn't crush him. He had healed many, and now all who suffered from diseases pressed around him to touch him. As he ministered, whenever the unclean spirits saw him, they fell down before him and cried out, "You are the Son of God!" But he strictly ordered them not to make him known.

Then he saw two boats by the lake and the fishermen had gone out of them and were washing their nets. He got into the boat that belonged to Simon and asked him to put out a little from the land. He sat down and taught the people

---

[43] Isaiah 42:1-3
[44]Mark 3:9-12; Luke 5:1-11

from the boat. When he finished, he said to Simon, "Head out to the deep, and let your nets down for a catch."

"Master, we worked hard all night and caught nothing." Simon answered. "But I will let the nets down if you say so."

They did and caught such a large number of fish that their nets were breaking. They signaled to their partners in the other boat to come and help them. They came and filled both boats so that they began to sink.

When Simon Peter saw it, he fell down at Jesus' knees, saying, "Leave me Lord, I am such a sinful man." He said this because he and all who were with him were astonished at the catch of fish, as were James and John, the sons of Zebedee, who were partners with Simon.

"Don't be afraid," Jesus said to Simon. "From now on you will be catching men."

The boats reached the shore, and they left everything and followed Jesus.

The Twelve and The Sermon

[45]During those days, he went out to the mountain to pray, and he prayed to God all night. When day came, he called his disciples to him, those whom he desired. From them he chose twelve and called them apostles. He appointed the twelve to be with him and also to send them out to preach and have authority to cast out demons.

The names of the twelve apostles are:

First, Simon (the one he named Peter),

Andrew his brother,

James and John (brothers and Zebedee's sons to whom he gave the name Boanerges or Sons of Thunder)

and Philip,

Bartholomew,

Matthew the tax collector,

Thomas,

James the son of Alphaeus,

Judas/Thaddaeus the son of James,

Simon the Cananaean (who was called the Zealot)

and Judas Iscariot, the traitor who betrayed him.

Jesus came down with them and stood on a level place on the mountain with a large crowd of his disciples and a great multitude of people from all Judea, Jerusalem, and the seacoast of Tyre and Sidon. They came to hear him and to be healed of their diseases. He also cured those who were troubled with unclean spirits. The whole crowd wanted to touch him because power came out of him and healed them all.

When he sat down, he looked at his disciples. Then he opened his mouth and taught them:

---

[45]Mark 3:13-19; Matthew 10:2-4; 5:1-7:29; Luke 6:12-49

"Blessed are you who are poor in spirit – you get the kingdom of God.

Blessed are those who mourn – they will be comforted.

Blessed are the meek – they inherit the earth.

Blessed are those who hunger and thirst for righteousness – they will be satisfied.

Blessed are you who weep now – you will laugh.

Blessed are the merciful – they will receive mercy.

Blessed are the pure in heart – they get to see God.

Blessed are the peacemakers – they will be called sons of God.

Blessed are those who are persecuted for righteousness' sake – the kingdom of Heaven belongs to them.

Blessed are you when people hate you and when they exclude you and revile you and spurn your name as evil and utter all kinds of evil against you falsely on account of the Son of Man. Rejoice in that day! Jump for joy! Look! Your reward in Heaven is great. They persecuted the prophets who were before you the same way."

"Woe to you who are rich – you have received your comfort.

Woe to you who are full now – you will be hungry.

Woe to you who laugh now – you will mourn and cry.

Woe to you when all people speak well of you – their fathers did the same to the false prophets."

"You are the salt of the earth, but if salt has lost its taste, how will it become salty again? It is good for nothing. Throw it out and let it be trampled under people's feet."

"You are the light of the world. A city set on a hill cannot be hidden, and people don't light a lamp and put it under a basket. Instead, they put it on a stand, and it gives light to everyone in the house. Let your light shine before others in the same way so they can see your good works and give glory to your heavenly Father."

"Don't think that I came to abolish the Law or the Prophets; I haven't come to abolish them but to fulfill them. The truth I am telling you is this: Until Heaven and Earth

37

pass away, not the smallest letter or part of a letter, will pass from the Law until it is accomplished."

"Therefore, whoever breaks one of the smallest of these commandments and teaches others to do the same will be called least in the kingdom of Heaven. But whoever obeys them and teaches them will be called great in the kingdom of Heaven. Because I tell you, unless your righteousness is greater than that of the scribes and Pharisees, you will never enter the kingdom of Heaven."

"You have heard that people were told long ago, 'You will not murder, and whoever murders will be judged.' Yet I say to you, everyone who is angry with his brother will be judged. Whoever insults his brother saying things like, 'You're worthless!' will be guilty before the council. And whoever says, 'You moron!' will be guilty enough to go into the fires of Hell."

"So if you are offering your gift at the altar and there remember that your brother has something against you, leave your gift at the altar and go. First, make things right with your brother, then come back and offer your gift."

"Work things out quickly with your accuser while you are going with him to court. Otherwise, your accuser will hand you over to the judge, and the judge to the guard, and you will be put in prison. Truly, I tell you, you will never get out until you have paid the last penny."

"You've heard the saying, 'You should not commit adultery,' but I tell you that everyone who looks at a woman and lusts has already committed adultery with her in his heart."

"If your right eye causes you to sin, gouge it out and throw it away. It's better to lose one part of your body than to have your whole body thrown into Hell. Also, if your right hand causes you to sin, cut it off and throw it away. It's better to lose one part of your body than for your whole body to go into Hell."

"It was also said, 'Whoever divorces his wife, let him give her divorce papers,' but I tell you that everyone who divorces his wife, except on the ground of sexual immorality, makes her commit adultery. Likewise, whoever marries a divorced woman commits adultery."

"Again you have heard that people were told long ago, 'You should not make false promises, but do whatever you promised before the Lord.' However, I say to you, don't make promises at all, either by Heaven because it is the throne of God or by the earth because it is his footstool or by Jerusalem because it is the city of the great King. And do not make a promise by your head because you cannot make one hair white or black. Let what you say be 'Yes' or 'No;' anything more comes from evil."

"You've heard the saying, 'An eye for an eye and a tooth for a tooth,' but I tell you, do not resist the one who is evil. Instead, if anyone slaps you on the right cheek, turn your other cheek to him also. If anyone sues you and takes your coat, let him have your clothes as well. If anyone forces you to go one mile, go two miles with him. If someone begs you, give to him, and don't say 'No' if someone wants to borrow from you. Don't demand your things back from the person who takes them. However you want others to treat you, treat them the same way."

"You've heard the saying, 'You should love your neighbor and hate your enemy,' but I tell whoever's listening, love your enemies, do good to those who hate you, bless those who curse you, and pray for those who persecute you. That's how you can be sons to your Father in Heaven. He makes his sun rise on the good and bad. He sends rain on the just and unjust. If you love those who love you, what reward will you get? Don't the tax collectors do that? Even sinners love those who love them. So what if you only greet your brothers; how is that better than others? Don't the Gentiles do that as well? If you do good to those who do good to you, what's the benefit to you? Sinners do the same thing. If you lend to people you expect to receive from, what credit is that to you? Even sinners lend to sinners to get back what they gave. Instead, love your enemies and do good. Lend, expecting nothing in return, and you will have a great reward. You will be sons of the Most High, for he is kind to the ungrateful and the evil. Therefore, you must be compassionate, just as your Father is compassionate, and complete, even as your heavenly Father is complete."

"Beware of showing off your righteousness before other people in order to be seen by them. If you do, you will get no reward from your Father who is in Heaven."

"When you give to the needy, don't blow a trumpet before you in the streets and synagogues as the hypocrites do. They do that so others will praise them. Truly, I say to you, that's all the reward they will get. But when you give to the needy, don't let your left hand know what your right hand is doing. That way you'll be giving in secret. Then your Father who sees secrets will reward you."

"Don't be like the hypocrites when you pray. They love to stand and pray in the synagogues and on the street corners so others will see them. Truly, I tell you, that's all the reward they will get. When you pray, go into your room and shut the door, and pray to your Father who is in secret. Then your Father who sees secrets will reward you."

"Also, when you pray, don't be repetitious like the Gentiles who think they will be heard by talking so much. Don't be like them because your Father knows what you need before you ask him. Pray like this:

"Our Father who is in Heaven,
hallowed be your name.
Your kingdom come,
your will be done,
on Earth as it is in Heaven.
Give us this day our daily bread
and forgive our sins
as we forgive those who sin against us.
Lead us not into temptation
but deliver us from evil."

"If you forgive the sins of others, your heavenly Father will also forgive you. But if you do not forgive the sins of others, your Father will not forgive your sins."

"When you fast, don't look miserable like the hypocrites, for they make obvious faces so other people will know they're fasting. The truth is – that is all the reward they'll get. But when you fast, anoint your head and wash your face so other people won't see you fasting, only your Father who sees secrets. Then your Father who sees secrets will reward you."

"Don't store up for yourselves treasures on Earth where moth and rust destroy and where thieves break in and steal. But store up for yourselves treasures in Heaven where moth and rust do not destroy and where thieves do not break in and steal. For where your treasure is, that's where your heart will be."

"The eye is the lamp in the body. If your eye is healthy, your whole body will be full of light, but if your eye is bad, your whole body will be full of darkness. And if the light in you is darkness, how great is the darkness!"

"No one can serve two masters. He will hate one and love the other, or he will be devoted to one and despise the other. You cannot serve God and money."

"This is why I tell you, don't worry about life – what you will eat or drink, or about your body, what you will put on. Life is more than food, right? And the body is more than clothing, right? Look at the birds of the air. They don't sow, reap, or gather into barns, yet your heavenly Father feeds them. Don't you think you are worth more than birds? Who can add a single hour to his span of life by worrying? Also, why are you anxious about clothes? Think about the lilies of the field and how they grow. They don't toil or spin, but I tell you, not even Solomon in all his glory was robed like one of these. If God is going to clothe the grass in the field, which is alive today and tomorrow is thrown into the oven, won't he clothe you so much better? O you of little faith! Don't worry and say, 'What are we going to eat?' or 'What are we going to drink?' or 'What are we going to wear?' The pagans focus on all these things, and indeed your heavenly Father already knows that you need them. Seek first the kingdom of God and his righteousness and all these things will be given to you. Don't worry about tomorrow. Tomorrow will worry about itself. Today has enough trouble of its own."

"Don't judge people, and you won't be judged; don't condemn people, and you won't be condemned. Forgive, and you will be forgiven. Give, and it will be given to you – plenty, pressed down, shaken together and running over, it will be poured into your lap. You will be judged the way you judge, and the measure you use will be measured back to you."

He also told them a parable: "Can a blind man lead a blind man? Won't they both fall into a pit? A student is not above his teacher, but all students when they are fully trained will be like their teacher."

"Why do you see the speck in your brother's eye but don't notice the log in your own eye? Or how can you say to your brother, 'Brother, let me take the speck out of your eye,' when you don't see the log that is in your own eye? You hypocrite, first take the log out of your eye, and then you can see clearly to take the speck out of your brother's eye."

"Do not give dogs what is holy, and do not throw your pearls before swine; they might trample them and turn to attack you."

"Ask, and it will be given to you. Seek, and you will find. Knock, and it will be opened to you. For everyone who asks, receives, and the one who seeks, finds, and to the one who knocks, it will be opened. Would any of you give your son a stone if he asked for bread? Or if he asked for a fish, would you give him a snake? If you then, who are bad, know how to give good gifts to your children, how much more will your heavenly Father give good things to those who ask him?"

"Whatever you want others to do to you, do the same to them. That is what the Law and the Prophets are about."

"Enter at the narrow gate because the gate is wide and the way is easy that leads to destruction, and many enter that way. However, the gate is narrow and the way is hard that leads to life, and only a few find it."

"Beware of false prophets who come to you in sheep's clothing, but on the inside are ravenous wolves. You will recognize them by their fruits. No good tree bears bad fruit, and no bad tree bears good fruit. Each tree is known by its own fruit. Do you get grapes from thorn bushes or figs from thistles? Every healthy tree bears good fruit, but the rotten tree bears bad fruit. Every tree that doesn't bear good fruit is cut down and thrown into the fire. You will recognize them by their fruits. In the same way, the good person produces good out of the good treasure of his heart, while the evil person produces evil out of his evil treasure. The mouth speaks what spills out of the heart."

"Not everyone who says to me, 'Lord, Lord,' will enter the kingdom of Heaven. Instead, it will be those who do the will of my Father in Heaven. On that day, many will say to me, 'Lord, Lord, didn't we prophesy in your name and cast out demons in your name and perform miracles in your name?' Then I will tell them, 'I never knew you. Get away from me you lawless workers.'"

"Why do you call me 'Lord, Lord,' but don't do what I tell you? Everyone who comes to me and hears my words and does them is like a wise man building a house. He dug deep and laid the foundation on the rock. The winds blew and the rain fell and the floods came and beat on that house, but it could not be shaken. It didn't fall because it had been built well on the rock. In contrast, everyone who hears my words and does not do them will be like a fool who built his house on the sand, without a foundation. The rain fell and the floods came and the winds blew and beat against that house, and immediately it fell with massive destruction."

When Jesus finished all his sayings, the people listening were astonished because he was teaching them as one who had authority, and the scribes didn't teach that way. And great crowds followed him as he came down from the mountain."

More Life in Galilee and Beyond

[46]Afterwards, he went to Capernaum, where there was a centurion with a servant who meant a lot to him, and the servant was sick and near death. When the centurion heard about Jesus, he sent Jewish elders to him, asking him to come and heal his servant. When they came to Jesus, they sincerely begged him, saying, "Lord, his servant is lying paralyzed at home in great suffering, and this centurion is worthy to have you help him because he loves our nation. In fact, he's the one who built our synagogue."

Then Jesus went with them, saying, "I will come and heal him."

When he was not far from the house, the centurion sent friends to speak for him: "Lord, don't trouble yourself. I'm not even worthy to have you under my roof. That's why I didn't presume to come to you, so just say the word and my servant will be healed. For I too am a man under authority with soldiers under me. I say to one, 'Go' and he goes, and to another, 'Come' and he comes, and to my servant, 'Do this' and he does it."

"Truly, I tell you all," Jesus marveled, "I have not found this kind of faith in anyone in Israel. I tell you, many will come from east and west and recline at the feast with Abraham, Isaac, and Jacob in the kingdom of Heaven, while the sons of the kingdom will be thrown into the darkness outside. In that place there will be weeping and gnashing of teeth."

"Go," he said. "Let it be done for you as you have believed." The servant was healed at that moment, and when the elders returned to the house, they found the servant well.

---

[46]Matthew 8:5-13; Luke 7:1-10

[47]Soon afterward he went to a town called Nain, and his disciples and a large crowd went with him. As he came close to the town gate, a dead man was being carried out. He was his widow mother's only son, and many from the town were with her. When the Lord saw her, he had compassion on her and said, "Don't cry." He went over and touched the casket, and the bearers stood still. Then he said, "Young man, I'm talking to you – get up."

At once the dead man sat up and began to talk, and Jesus gave him back to his mother. It scared everyone and they honored God, saying, "A mighty prophet has arisen among us!" and "God has visited his people!" Of course, this news about him spread throughout Judea and all the surrounding country.

[48]Meanwhile, John was in prison, and when John's disciples told him all that Jesus was doing, he sent word to the Lord by two of his disciples. When the men arrived they said, "John the Baptizer has sent us to ask you, 'Are you the one who is to come, or should we look for someone else?'"

During the time they were there, he healed many people of diseases and plagues and evil spirits; he even gave sight to the blind.

"Go and tell John what you see and hear," Jesus told them. "[49]*The blind receive sight*, the lame walk, lepers are cleansed, the deaf hear, the dead are raised, *and the poor enjoy good news*. Also, blessed is the one who is not offended by me."

When John's messengers left, Jesus began to talk to the crowds about him saying, "What did you go to see in the wilderness – a reed shaken by the wind? What did you go out to see? A man dressed in fine clothes? Look, those who live in luxury wearing soft expensive clothes are in kings' houses.

---

[47] Luke 7:11-17
[48]Matthew 11:2-19, Luke 7:18-35
[49] Isaiah 35:5; 61:1

Then what did you go out to see? A prophet? That's right, and more than a prophet. This Scripture is written about him: [50]*Behold! I send my messenger before you and he will prepare the way in front of you.* To tell you the truth, among those born of women, no one greater than John the Baptizer has stood up. Yet the one who is least in the kingdom of God is greater than John. From the days of John the Baptizer until now, the kingdom of Heaven has suffered violence, and the aggressive must force their way into it. All the Prophets and the Law prophesied until John, and if you are open to it, he is Elijah who was prophesied to come. He who has ears to hear, let him hear."

When everyone heard this, including the tax collectors, they said, "God is just." They had also been immersed with the baptism of John, but the Pharisees and the Lawyers refused to be immersed by John because they rejected God's purpose for them.

Jesus continued, "To what would I compare the people of this generation? What are they like? They're like children sitting in the marketplaces complaining to their playmates, 'We played the flute for you and you didn't dance; we sang a dirge and you didn't mourn.' I say this because John the Baptizer has come, and he doesn't eat any bread or drink any wine, and you say, 'He has a demon.' Whereas the Son of Man has come eating and drinking, and you say, 'Look at him! A glutton and a drunk, a friend of tax collectors and sinners!' Yet wisdom is justified by all her children and their deeds."

[51]Jesus began to denounce the cities where most of his miracles had been done because they did not repent. "Woe to you Chorazin! Woe to you Bethsaida! If the miracles done in you had been done in Tyre and Sidon, they would have repented a long time ago in sackcloth and ashes. But I tell

---

[50] Malachi 3:1
[51]Matthew 11:20-24; Luke 7:36-50

you, it will be more bearable on judgment day for Tyre and Sidon than for you. As for you Capernaum, will you go to Heaven? You're going to Hell! If the miracles done in you had been done in Sodom, it would still be here today. I tell you that it will be more tolerable on judgment day for the land of Sodom than for you."

Then one of the Pharisees invited Jesus to eat with him, so he went to the Pharisee's house and took his place at the table. When a local woman, who was a sinner, learned that Jesus was reclining at the table in the Pharisee's house, she brought an alabaster flask of perfumed oil and stood behind him at his feet, weeping. As her tears wet his feet, she wiped them with her hair and kissed his feet and anointed them with the perfume.

When the Pharisee who had invited him saw this, he said to himself, "If this man were a prophet he'd know what kind of woman is touching him – she's a sinner."

"Simon, I have something to say to you," Jesus said.

"Say it, teacher."

"A certain lender had two debtors. One owed five hundred silver coins and the other fifty. When they couldn't pay, he canceled both debts. Now which one will love him more?"

"I suppose it will be the one who had the bigger debt written off," he answered.

"You're right," Jesus replied as he turned to the woman and said to Simon, "Do you see this woman? I came into your house, and you gave me no water for my feet, but she has wet my feet with her tears and wiped them with her hair. You didn't greet me with a kiss, but from the time I came in, she hasn't stopped kissing my feet. You didn't anoint my head with oil, but she has anointed my feet with perfumed oil. Let me tell you, her sins – and she has many – are forgiven because she loves so much. You see, the one who is forgiven little, loves little."

He turned to her and said, "Your sins are forgiven."

Those who were at the table with him began to talk among themselves saying, "Who is this? He can forgive sins?"

Jesus continued speaking to the woman, "Your faith has saved you. Go in peace."

[52]Soon afterward, he went on through cities and villages, bringing the good news of the kingdom of God. The twelve were with him as well as some women who had been healed of evil spirits and infirmities. These women included Mary, called Magdalene, who had seven demons leave her, and Joanna, the wife of Chuza – Herod's household manager. Along with them, Susanna and many others provided for them out of their means.

[53]Later, he went home and the crowd gathered again. A demon-oppressed man who was blind and mute was brought to him, and he healed him by casting out the mute demon so that the man could see and talk. Everyone marveled, "Can this be the Son of David?"

However, when some of the Pharisees and the scribes who came down from Jerusalem heard it, they were saying, "He's possessed by Beelzebul" and "He casts out the demons using the prince of demons." Others kept asking him for a sign from Heaven in order to test him.

He knew what they were thinking, and he called them over and said to them in parables, "How can Satan cast out Satan? If a kingdom is divided against itself, that kingdom cannot stand – it will fall. If a house is divided against itself, that house won't stand, and if Satan has risen up against himself and casts out Satan, he cannot stand divided – he's coming to an end! How will his kingdom stand? You say I cast out demons by Beelzebul. If I do, who's helping these sons of yours cast them out? Therefore, they will be your judges. And if it's by God's finger or by his Spirit that I cast out demons, then the kingdom of God is all around you.

---

[52]Luke 8:1-3
[53] Mark 3:20-35; Matthew 12:22-50; Luke 11:14-36; 8:19-21

When a fully armed strong man guards his own palace, his things are safe. But when someone stronger attacks him and binds the strong man, he takes away his trusted armor. He can certainly plunder his house and divide his spoil. Whoever is not with me is against me, and whoever does not gather with me, scatters."

"The truth is – the children of man will be forgiven all sins and whatever blasphemies they speak, but whoever blasphemes against the Holy Spirit will not have forgiveness – they are guilty of a lasting sin. Whoever speaks a word against the Son of Man will be forgiven, but whoever speaks against the Holy Spirit will not be forgiven, either in this age or in the age to come." He said this because they claimed, "He has an unclean spirit."

Jesus continued, "When the unclean spirit has gone out of a person, it moves through waterless places seeking rest. When it doesn't find any, it says, 'I will go back to my house that I left.' It returns, finds the house empty, swept, and in order. Then it leaves and brings seven other spirits more evil than itself, and they go inside to live there. It makes the last state of that person worse than the first. It's going to be the same way with this evil generation."

"You can make the tree good, and its fruit will be good, or you can make the tree bad, and its fruit will be bad. The tree will be identified by its fruit. You den of vipers! How can you speak good when you are evil? The mouth speaks from what pours out of the heart. The good person brings good out of his good treasure, and the evil person brings evil out of his evil treasure. I tell you, on judgment day, people will answer for every careless word they speak because you will be justified by your words and you will be condemned by your words."

The crowds were sitting around Jesus, growing so large that he and the disciples couldn't even eat. His mother and his brothers heard about it, and they went out to seize him. "He's out of his mind," the family was saying. They came and stood outside and sent others to ask if they could speak to him. "Your mother and your brothers are outside, looking for you," someone told him.

"Who are my mother and my brothers?" he answered.

Looking around at those seated, he stretched out his hand toward his disciples and said, "Here are my mother and my brothers. Whoever does the will of God, my father in Heaven, he is my brother and sister and mother."

As he said these things, a woman in the crowd spoke up and said to him, "Blessed is the womb that bore you and the breasts you nursed from!"

"Blessed rather are those who hear the word of God and keep it," Jesus replied.

Some of the scribes and Pharisees answered him, "Teacher, we want to see you do a miracle."

"This generation is an evil and adulterous generation," he answered. "It looks for a sign, but no sign will be given to it except the sign of the prophet Jonah. Just as Jonah became a sign to the people of Nineveh and was in the belly of the great fish three days and nights, so will the Son of Man be three days and nights in the heart of the earth. The men of Nineveh will rise up at the judgment with this generation and condemn it because they repented when Jonah preached, and look, something greater than Jonah is here. The queen of the South will also rise up at the judgment with this generation and condemn it, for she came from the ends of the earth to hear Solomon's wisdom, and look, something greater than Solomon is here."

"No one lights a lamp and puts it in a cellar or under a basket. They put it on a stand so those who come in may see the light. Your eye is the lamp of your body. When your eye is healthy, your whole body is full of light. But when it's bad, your body is full of darkness. You need to be careful or the light in you will be darkness. If your whole body is full of light, with no dark parts, it will be all bright like when a lamp gives you light with its rays."

[54]Again that same day, Jesus went out of the house, sat by the sea and began to teach. A very large crowd gathered from several towns, so he got into a boat and sat in it on the sea as the crowd stood on the beach. Using parables, he taught them many things.

"Listen!" he said. "A farmer went out to sow. As he sowed, some seed fell on the path and was trampled underfoot. The birds flying around came and ate it. Other seed fell on rocky ground where there was not much soil. It sprouted too quickly since it had no depth of soil, and when the sun came up, it was scorched and withered because it didn't have roots or water. Other seed fell among thorns, which grew up with the seed and choked it, and it produced no grain. Still, other seed fell into good soil. It produced grain, growing and multiplying and producing thirty, sixty, and a hundred times as much. He who has ears to hear, let him hear."

Later when he was with the twelve and some others, they wanted to know what this parable meant. They also asked Jesus, "Why do you speak to them in parables?"

"You've been given the ability to understand the mystery of the kingdom of God. Those outside have not, so everything is in parables." He continued, "The one who has this ability will be given more, and he will have more than enough, but the one who doesn't have this ability, even what he has will be taken away. Here's the reason I speak to them in parables – because they look but do not see, and they listen but do not hear or understand. Certainly, in their case, the prophecy of Isaiah is fulfilled that says:

[55]You will definitely hear but never understand,
and you will indeed see but never perceive.
Because this people's heart has grown dull,
and with their ears they can barely hear,

---

[54]Mark 4:1-20; Matthew 13:1-30; Luke 8:4-15
[55] Isaiah 6:9-10; Psalm 119:70; Zechariah 7:11

and they have closed their eyes,
so they won't see with their eyes
and hear with their ears,
and understand with their heart,
and turn, and I would heal them,
and they would be forgiven.

"But blessed are your eyes because they see and your ears because they hear. Truly, I tell you, many prophets and righteous people longed to see what you see and did not see it and to hear what you hear and did not hear it."

He also said, "You don't understand this parable? Then how will you understand any of the parables? Listen again to the parable of the farmer:

"The seed is the word of God. The farmer sows the word. Some people are like the seed along the path where the word is sown in them. They hear the word of the kingdom but don't understand it because Satan immediately comes and takes away the word so they won't believe and be saved. Others are like the ones sown on rocky ground. They hear the word and instantly receive it with joy. But they don't have roots, so they endure and believe for a while, yet they fall away as soon as hard times or persecutions come because of the word."

"Still others are like the ones sown among thorns. They hear the word, but the cares of the world and the deceitfulness of riches and other desires come in and choke the word, making it unfruitful. However, those sown on the good soil are the ones who hear the word, understand and accept it, then hold on to it with an honest and good heart. They surely bear fruit with endurance and produce a crop thirty, sixty, or a hundred times as much."

He shared another parable with them, saying, "The kingdom of Heaven can be compared to a man who planted good seed in his field, but his enemy came and planted weeds among the wheat and snuck away while his men were sleeping. When the plants came up and bore grain, the weeds grew as well. Then the servants of the master came and said to him, 'Master, didn't you plant good seed in your field? Why are there weeds?'

'An enemy has done this,' he answered.

'Do you want us to go and gather them?' they asked.

'No,' he said, 'because in gathering the weeds you might pull up the wheat along with them. Let both grow together until harvest time, and then I will tell the reapers to gather the weeds first and tie them in bundles to be burned, but gather the wheat into my barn.'"

[56]Jesus also said to them, "Do you bring a lamp in to put it under a basket or jar or bed? No one lights a lamp and covers it. Instead, they put it on a stand and all who come in may see the light. Nothing is hidden that will not be revealed, nor is anything secret that will not be known and come to light. If anyone has ears to hear, let him hear."

And he said, "Pay attention to what you hear, for the measure you use will be measured to you, and more than that because to the one who has, more will be given, and to the one who has not, even what he thinks he has will be taken away."

He continued, "The kingdom of God is like a man who scatters seed on the ground. He sleeps and rises night and day, and the seed sprouts and grows – he doesn't know how. The earth produces by itself, first the shoot, then the ear, then the full grain in the ear. When the grain is ripe, he uses the sickle right away because the harvest has come."

He shared still another parable with them, saying, "What can we compare the kingdom of God to, or what story can we use for it? The kingdom of Heaven is like a grain of mustard seed that a man took and planted in his field. It's smaller than all the seeds on Earth, but planted, it grows up and becomes larger than all the garden plants with large branches. It becomes a tree, and the birds can make nests in its branches."

---

[56]Mark 4:21-34; Matthew 13:31-52; Luke 8:16-18

He told them another parable: "The kingdom of Heaven is like yeast that a woman took and hid in a bushel of flour until it was all leavened."

He used many stories like this to speak the word to the crowds as they were able to hear it. He did not speak to them without a parable, but privately he explained everything to his disciples. This fulfilled what the prophet said: [57]*I will open my mouth in parables; I will speak what has been hidden since the foundation of the world.*

Then he left the crowds and went into the house. His disciples also came, saying, "Explain to us the parable about the weeds in the field."

"The one who sows the good seed is the Son of Man," he began. "The field is the world, and the good seed represents the children of the kingdom. The weeds are the sons of the evil one, and the enemy who planted them is the Devil. The harvest is the end of the age, and the harvesters are angels. Just as the weeds are gathered and burned with fire, it will be the same at the end of the age. The Son of Man will send his angels to pull all causes of sin and all law-breakers out of his kingdom and throw them into the fiery furnace where they will weep and gnash their teeth. And the righteous will shine like the sun in their Father's kingdom. He who has ears, let him hear."

"The kingdom of Heaven is like treasure hidden in a field that a man found and covered up. He was so happy that he went and sold everything he had and bought that field."

"Again, the kingdom of Heaven is like a merchant in search of fine pearls, and when he found one pearl that was highly valuable, he went and sold everything he had and bought it."

"And the kingdom of Heaven is like a net that was thrown into the sea and gathered all kinds of fish. When it was full, men pulled it ashore and sat down and sorted the

---

[57] Psalm 78:2

good fish into buckets but threw away the bad. It will be the same way at the close of the age. The angels will come out and separate the evil from the righteous and throw them into the fiery furnace. In that place there will be weeping and gnashing of teeth. Have you understood all these things?"

They said, "Yes."

He continued, "Every scribe who has been trained for the kingdom of Heaven is like a master of a house who brings out of his treasure things that are new and things that are old."

[58]Although Jesus had finished storying that evening, a crowd continued to gather. He said, "Let's go to the other side of the lake."

As they traveled along the road, a scribe said, "Teacher, I will follow you wherever you go."

"Foxes have holes and birds of the air have nests, but the Son of Man doesn't have a place to lay his head," Jesus replied.

Then he said to another disciple, "Follow me."

"Lord," he replied, "I need to go and bury my father first."

"Let the dead bury their dead," said Jesus, "but you go tell people about the kingdom of God."

Another said, "I will follow you Lord, but let me say goodbye back home."

"No one who puts his hand to the plow and looks back is fit for the kingdom of God," Jesus told him.

After leaving the crowd, the disciples took Jesus with them in the boat, just as he was. Other boats were with him as well. As they sailed, he fell asleep, and a powerful windstorm came down on the lake, breaking the waves over into the boat and filling it up. They were in danger, but he was in the back, sleeping on a cushion.

They woke him up shouting, "Master! Master!"

---

[58]Mark 4:35-41, 5:1-20; Matthew 13:53, 8:18-34; Lk 8:22-39, 9:57-62

"Teacher!"

"Save us Lord!"

"Don't you care that we're dying?"

"Why are you afraid?" he said. "What small faith." Then he rebuked the wind and raging waves and said to the sea, "Hush! Be still!"

The wind ceased and all was calm. He said, "Why are you so afraid? Where is your faith? You still don't have any?"

They were scared and marveling to one other, "Who is this that he commands and even the wind and the sea obey him?"

They sailed on and came to the other side of the sea to the region of the Gerasenes and Gadarenes, which is opposite Galilee. As soon as Jesus had stepped out of the boat, two demon-possessed men from the city came out from the tombs and met them. They were so mean that no one could pass by that way.

For a long time, one of the men had not worn clothes or lived in a house; he lived among the tombs. No one could restrain him anymore, although he had often been shackled and chained and kept under guard. But the demons possessed him and he tore the chains apart and broke the shackles in pieces. No one had the strength to hold him, and the demons would drive him into the desert. Night and day, among the tombs and on the mountains, he was always screaming and bruising himself with stones.

When he saw Jesus from far off, he ran and fell down before him crying out with a loud voice, "WHAT DO YOU WANT WITH ME JESUS, SON OF THE MOST HIGH GOD? BY GOD I DEMAND – DON'T TORMENT ME!"

Jesus had already commanded, "Come out of the man you filthy spirit!"

"WHAT DO YOU WANT WITH US, O SON OF GOD?" they screamed. "HAVE YOU COME HERE TO TORMENT US BEFORE THE TIME?"

"What is your name?" Jesus inquired.

"My name is Legion, for we are many." (He said this because many demons had entered the man.) Desperately, they begged him not to force them out of the country or into the abyss.

There was a large herd of pigs feeding nearby on the hillside, and the demons begged Jesus, "If you cast us out, let us enter the herd of pigs."

"Go," he said.

The demons came out of the men and entered the pigs, and the herd of about two thousand stampeded down the steep bank and drowned in the lake.

When the herdsmen saw what had happened, they ran and told the whole story all around town.

Everyone in the city came to meet Jesus and see what had happened. They found the man, exorcised of the legion of demons, sitting at the feet of Jesus. He had on clothes and was in his right mind, which scared them. Those who saw what happened to the demon-possessed man and to the pigs recounted the events, causing all the people around Gerasa to become so afraid that they began to beg Jesus to leave them.

As Jesus was getting into the boat, the man begged to go with him, but he wouldn't let him. Instead, Jesus sent him away. "Go home to your friends," he said, "and tell them how much the Lord God has done for you. Tell them how he had mercy on you."

The healed man left and visited the cities of the Decapolis telling the people there how much Jesus had done for him, and everyone marveled.

[59]When Jesus had crossed back over in the boat to his own city Capernaum, a large crowd was waiting to welcome him beside the sea.

John's disciples and the Pharisees were fasting, and the disciples of John came to him, saying, "Why do we and the

---

[59] Mark 2:18-22; Matthew 9:14-17; Luke 5:33-39

Pharisees' disciples fast often, but your disciples don't fast? Yours eat and drink."

"Can the wedding guests mourn and fast while the bridegroom is with them?" Jesus questioned. Then he answered them, "As long as they have the bridegroom with them, they cannot fast, but the days will come when the bridegroom is taken away from them. They will fast in that day."

He also told them a parable: "No one takes a piece from a new, unshrunk cloth, and sews it onto an old garment. If he does, the new patch tears away from the old and a worse tear is made. And no one puts new wine into old wineskins. If he does, the new wine will burst the skins and both the wine and the skins are lost. Instead, new wine must be put into fresh wineskins. No one after drinking old wine desires the new wine: 'The old is good enough,' they say."

+ + +

[60]Jairus, a ruler of the synagogue also came to Jesus. He had an only daughter, about twelve years old, and she was dying. When he saw Jesus, he fell at his feet and begged him to come to his house, pleading, "My little daughter is nearly dead or she may already be dead by now. Come lay your hands on her so that she may be healed and live." So Jesus and his disciples got up and followed him.

The masses were following him closely, and among the group was a woman who had been afflicted with bleeding for twelve years. Although she had many different doctors over the years, she still suffered and none of them had made her well. She was in financial ruin, yet was still no better physically. She actually grew worse.

She had heard the reports about Jesus, and she came up behind him in the crowd and touched the fringe of his

---

[60]Mark 5:21-43; Matthew 9:18-38; Luke 8:40-56

clothes, thinking, "If I can only touch his clothes, I'll be healed."

Immediately the bleeding stopped, and she felt inside that she was healed of her disease.

Jesus, without hesitation, turned around in the crowd and asked, "Who touched my clothes?"

When everyone denied it, Peter and his disciples said to him, "Master, the crowds are surrounding and pressing against you! And you're asking, 'Who touched me'?"

"I know someone touched me," said Jesus, looking around to see who had done it, "because power has gone out from me."

When the woman saw that she couldn't hide, she came and fell down in front of him. She was afraid and shaking as she admitted before everyone why she had touched him. She also told them that she was healed immediately. As he looked at her he said, "Take heart, daughter, you're well because of your faith. Go in peace and be healed of your disease."

While he was still speaking, some people came from the ruler's house to say, "Your daughter is dead. Why trouble the teacher anymore?"

Overhearing them, Jesus said to the ruler of the synagogue, "Don't be afraid. Just believe and she'll be alright." Jesus wouldn't allow anyone to follow him except Peter and the brothers, James and John. They came to the house of the ruler of the synagogue, and Jesus saw the flute players and a cluster of people weeping and wailing loudly.

When he came in, he said, "Why all this weeping and carrying on? Stop crying and go away. The child isn't dead – she's sleeping."

They knew she was dead, so they began to laugh at him. He put them all out and took the child's father and mother, along with those who were with him – Peter, James, and John – and went in to see the child. He took her by the hand and called to her, "Talitha koom," which means, "Little girl, I'm talking to you – now get up."

Right away her spirit returned. The twelve year old got up and started walking, and they were overwhelmed with amazement. Jesus asked that she be fed and he also demanded that they tell no one what had happened. However, the news spread all around.

As Jesus traveled on from there, two blind men followed him, crying out loudly, "Have mercy on us, Son of David."

When he entered the house, the blind men came to him and Jesus asked them, "Do you believe that I can do this?"

"Yes sir," they answered.

He touched their eyes and said, "Let your faith decide what you receive." At that moment they could see!

"Don't tell a soul about this," Jesus strongly demanded. But they left and told the story all over the place.

Incredibly, as they were leaving, a demon possessed man who was mute was brought to him, and when the demon had been cast out, the mute man began talking. Everyone cheered in amazement, "Nothing like this ever happens in Israel!"

But the Pharisees maintained, "He casts out demons by the prince of demons."

Jesus continued to travel through all the cities and villages, teaching in their synagogues, declaring the good news of the kingdom, and healing every sickness and disease. When he saw the crowds, he was moved with compassion because they were abused and scattered, like sheep without a shepherd. "The harvest is full," he said to his followers, "but the workers are few. Pray earnestly to the Lord to send workers into his harvest."

[61]His disciples followed him to his hometown Nazareth where he taught in the synagogue on the Sabbath as he customarily did. They handed him the scroll of the prophet Isaiah as he stood up to read. He opened the scroll and found the place where it was written:

---

[61]Mark 6:1-6; Matthew 13:54-58; Luke 4:16-30

[62]The Spirit of the Lord is on me because he has anointed me to tell the gospel to the poor. He sent me to heal the brokenhearted, preach deliverance to the captives, recovery of sight to the blind, and set the oppressed free. I am here to tell everyone that this is the year of Yahweh's favor.

He closed the book and gave it back to the attendant and sat down. All eyes in the synagogue were on him. He said, "Today as you listened, this Scripture was fulfilled."

Many were listening and were astonished. They all spoke highly of him and marveled at the gracious words that came out of his mouth. They said, "Where did this man get these things?"

"What about this wisdom that he's been given?"

"How can his hands do all these miracles?"

"Isn't this the carpenter, the son of Mary and Joseph, and brother of James and Joses and Judas and Simon? Aren't all his sisters here with us?"

Jesus told them, "Without a doubt you will quote this proverb to me, 'Doctor, heal yourself.' You'll say, 'We have heard what you did at Capernaum. Do the same things here in your hometown.'"

They got mad at him, so Jesus said, "A prophet is not dishonored, except in his hometown among his relatives, and in his own house. It's also true that there were many widows in Israel during the time of Elijah when the heavens were shut up three years and six months, and there came a great famine over all the land. Yet Elijah wasn't sent to any of them, but only to Zarephath in the land of Sidon to a widow woman. There were also many lepers in Israel in the time of Elisha the prophet, and none of them were cleansed, except Naaman the Syrian."

The people in the synagogue were enraged as they heard these things, and they got up and drove him out of the city to a cliff on which their city was built. They wanted

---

[62] Isaiah 61:1-2

to throw him off, but he passed through the middle of them and went away.

As a result of their unbelief, Jesus couldn't do any miracles there, except that he laid his hands on a few sick people and healed them. Their disbelief amazed him. So he just went through the villages teaching.

[63]Later he called the twelve disciples to himself and began to send them out two by two. He sent them out to declare the kingdom of God and gave them power and authority over all demons. They were to cast them out and heal every sickness and disease. He commanded that they take nothing with them for their journey except a staff, but no bread, no pack, no money in their belts, and no extra shirt. They were to wear sandals.

"Don't go anywhere among the Gentiles or into any Samaritan town. Go only to the lost sheep of the house of Israel, and spread the word as you go, saying, 'The kingdom of Heaven is so close.' Heal the sick, raise the dead, cleanse lepers, and cast out demons. You received without paying, give without charging. Do not accept gold, silver, or copper for your belts. Do not accept a bag during your journey nor extra undergarments, extra sandals, or extra staff because the laborer deserves his food."

"Find out who is worthy in the towns and villages you enter and stay there until you leave. Whatever house you visit, greet it and let your peace come upon it if the house is worthy. Otherwise, let your peace return to you. Likewise, when you leave that house or town, shake off the dust from your feet as a testimony against any place that will not welcome you and listen to what you have to say. I'm telling you, it will be more bearable on judgment day for the land of Sodom and Gomorrah than for that town."

"Listen, I'm sending you out like sheep among wolves, so be wise as snakes and innocent as doves. Keep your guard

---

[63]Mark 6:7-13; Matthew 10:1,5-11:1; Luke 9:1-6

up, for they will take you to court and beat you in their synagogues. Because of me, you will be dragged before governors and kings to bear witness before them and before the Gentiles."

"When they hand you over, don't worry about how you should speak or what you should say, that will all be given to you when it's time. It won't be you talking, but your Father's Spirit speaking through you.

Know that brother will hand over brother to death, father will denounce his child, and children will rise up against parents and have them put to death. You will be hated by all because of me. Also know that the one who endures to the end will be saved. When they persecute you in one town, run to the next. I'm telling the truth when I say that the Son of Man will come before you have made it through all the towns of Israel."

"A student is not superior to his teacher, neither is a servant above his master. Satisfaction is the student being like his teacher and the servant like his master. And if they have called the master of the house Beelzebul, what worse names will they use for his family?"

"Don't be afraid of them since nothing is covered that won't be revealed or hidden that will not be made known. What I tell you in the dark, say it in the light; what is whispered in your ear, shout it from the housetops. Don't fear those who kill the body but have no power to kill the soul. Instead, you should fear the one who can destroy both soul and body in Hell. Aren't two sparrows sold for a penny? And not one of them will fall to the ground without your Father's say-so. Even the hairs of your head are all numbered. Therefore, don't be afraid; you're worth more than many sparrows. Everyone who confesses me before men, I will also confess before my Father who is in Heaven. Whoever denies me before men, I will also deny before my Father who is in Heaven."

"Don't think that I've come to bring peace to the earth. I have not come to bring peace, but a sword. I've come to set

[64]*a man against his father, and a daughter against her mother, and a daughter-in-law against her mother-in-law; a person's enemies will be those of his own household."*

"Whoever loves father or mother more than me is not worthy of me, and whoever loves son or daughter more than me is not worthy of me. Whoever does not take his cross and follow me is not worthy of me. Whoever finds his life will lose it, and whoever loses his life for my sake will find it."

"Whoever receives you receives me, and whoever receives me receives him who sent me. The one who receives a prophet because he is a prophet will receive a prophet's reward, and the one who receives a righteous person because he is a righteous person will receive a righteous person's reward. Truly I tell you, whoever gives one of these little ones even a cup of cold water because he is a disciple, he will by no means lose his reward."

When Jesus had finished instructing his twelve disciples, they went out and proclaimed that people should repent, and they healed many people, casting out demons, and anointing the sick with oil as they healed them. Jesus also went on from there to teach and preach in their cities.

[65]At that time, King Herod, the tetrarch, heard about the fame of Jesus and all that was happening. He was perplexed, and he told his servants, "This is John the Baptizer, the one I beheaded. He's been raised from the dead; that's why these miraculous powers are at work in him."

Others disagreed saying, "He is Elijah," while others proclaimed, "He is a risen prophet, like one of the prophets of old."

Herod said, "I beheaded John, but who is this man I hear so much about?" And he tried to see Jesus.

Before all this, Herod had seized John, bound him, and put him in prison for the sake of Herodias, his brother

---

[64] Micah 7:6
[65] Mark 6:14-29; Matthew 14:1-12; Luke 9:7-9

Philip's wife. Because Herod had married her, John had been saying to him, "It is not lawful for you to have your brother's wife."

So Herodias had a grudge against John and wanted to put him to death, but was unable to because Herod wouldn't let her. Herod wished to kill John as well, but he was afraid of him, and he feared the people because they thought John was a prophet. Therefore, since Herod knew that he was a righteous and holy man, he kept him safe. When he listened to John, he was greatly perplexed, but he gladly listened to him.

One day Herodias seized her opportunity. It was Herod's birthday, and he held a banquet for his nobles, military commanders, and the leading men of Galilee. When Herodias' daughter came in and danced, she pleased Herod and his guests so much that the king said to the girl, "Ask me for whatever you wish and I will give it to you." He even vowed to her, "Whatever you ask for is yours, up to half of my kingdom."

She stepped out and asked her mother, "What should I ask for?"

"The head of John the Baptizer," she said.

Herodias returned in a hurry to the king and answered, "I want you to give me the head of John the Baptizer on a platter – right now."

The king was deeply sorry, but he knew he couldn't break his oaths in front of his guests. Right then, the king sent an executioner with orders to bring John's head. He went and beheaded him in the prison and brought his head on a platter and gave it to the girl, and the girl gave it to her mother. When his disciples heard about it, they came and took his body and laid it in a tomb.

[66]They returned to Jesus and told him about John and about all they had accomplished and taught after he had sent

---

[66]Mark 6:30-45; Matthew 14:13-22; Luke 9:10-17; John 6:1-15

them out. Still, many were coming and going, and they had couldn't rest, even to eat. Jesus said, "Come away by yourselves to a quiet place and rest a while." Then they left in the boat to get away alone to a desolate place. They arrived at the other side of the Sea of Galilee, which is the Sea of Tiberias to a town called Bethsaida.

A large crowd was following him because they saw the miracles and signs he was doing for the sick, and they ran there on foot from all the towns and arrived ahead of them. When he went ashore he saw a great crowd, and he had compassion on them because they were like sheep without a shepherd.

Jesus told them about the kingdom of God, taught them many things, and cured those who needed healing. This happened at the time of the Passover, and Jesus went up on the mountain and sat down with his disciples. As it grew late, his disciples came to him and said, "It's late and we're in the middle of nowhere. Send these people away so they can go into the countryside and villages to buy food and find a place to stay."

"They don't need to leave," Jesus said as he looked up at the large crowd coming toward him. "You feed them."

Then Jesus said to Philip, "Where can we buy bread to feed these people?"

Jesus knew what he was going to do, but he asked this to test him. Philip answered, "Two hundred days wages would not buy enough bread for them all to have even a little bit."

Still, the disciples asked, "Do you want us to go and buy it?"

"How many loaves do you already have?" Jesus asked. "Go and see."

His disciple Andrew, Simon Peter's brother, told him, "There's a boy here who has five barley loaves and two fish, but what good is that for this many?"

Jesus said, "Bring them to me and have the people sit down on the grass in groups of about fifty each." The place had a lot of grass and they sat down in groups, by hundreds and by fifties.

Jesus took the five loaves, looked up to Heaven, gave thanks, and said a blessing over them. He broke the loaves and gave them to the disciples, and the disciples gave them to the crowds. He did the same with the two fish. And he let the people have as much as they wanted. When they were satisfied and full, he told his disciples, "Gather up the leftovers; don't waste anything."

They gathered them up and filled twelve baskets with the leftovers from the fish and the five barley loaves eaten by about five thousand men, not counting the women and children.

When the people saw the sign that he had done, they said, "This is definitely the Prophet who is to come into the world!"

Jesus quickly perceived that they were about to come and take him by force and make him king. Immediately, he made his disciples go down to the sea and leave in the boat without him. They were heading to the other side of Bethsaida toward Capernaum, while he dismissed the crowd.

[67]He left them and went up on the mountain by himself to pray. When evening came, he was there alone. By this time, the boat was a long way from the land, beaten by the waves, with the sea and the wind raging against them. After rowing about three or four miles, it had grown dark and Jesus had not come to them. Jesus could see how hard it was for them to make any headway.

It was between 3:00 and 6:00 a.m. when he came to them, walking on the sea. He intended to walk right past them, but when they all saw him walking on the sea and coming near the boat, they were terrified and yelling, "IT'S A GHOST!"

---

[67]Mark 6:46-56; Matthew 14:23-36; John 6:16-21

Jesus spoke to them immediately and said, "Don't worry; it's me. Don't be afraid."

Peter responded, "Lord, if it's you, command me to come to you on the water."

"Come on," he said.

And Peter got out of the boat and walked on the water. He came to Jesus, but when he saw the wind, he was afraid and started sinking and crying out, "Lord, save me!"

Jesus reached out his hand and took hold of him, saying, "O you of little faith, why did you doubt?"

Then the disciples were glad to take Jesus into the boat. When they got in, the wind ceased and instantly the boat was at the land where they wanted to arrive. And they worshiped Jesus there, saying, "Truly you are the Son of God." Still, they were utterly astounded; their hearts were hard, so they didn't even understand about the loaves.

Now they had landed at Gennesaret and moored to the shore. When they got out of the boat, the people recognized Jesus right away and ran about the whole region bringing back sick people on their beds to wherever they heard he was. Everywhere he went, in villages, cities, or the countryside, they laid the sick in the marketplaces and begged to touch even the hem of his garment. Everyone who touched it was made well.

[68]The next day, the crowd that remained on the other side of the sea noticed there had been only one boat and that Jesus hadn't entered the boat with his disciples. Instead, they had gone away alone.

Other boats from Tiberias came near the place where they had eaten the bread after the Lord had given thanks. When the crowd saw that neither Jesus nor his disciples were there, they got back into the boats and went to Capernaum to find Jesus.

---

[68]John 6:22-71

They found him on the other side of the sea, and they said to him, "Rabbi, when did you get here?"

Jesus answered, "The truth is – you're seeking me not because you saw signs, but because you ate all the bread you wanted. Do not work for the food that perishes but for the food that endures to life in the coming age. The Son of Man can give you that food because God the Father guarantees him."

Then they wanted to know, "What must we do to do the works of God?"

"This is the work of God – believe in the one God has sent."

Still they asked, "What miraculous sign do you do that we may see and believe you? What will you do? Our fathers ate the manna in the wilderness, it's even written: [69]*He gave them bread from Heaven to eat.*"

Jesus answered, "The truth is – Moses did not give you the bread from Heaven, but my Father gives you the true bread from Heaven. The bread of God is he who comes down from Heaven and gives life to the world."

They said to him, "Sir, give us this bread from now on."

"I am the bread of life," Jesus said. "Whoever comes to me will not hunger, and whoever believes in me will never thirst. I told you that you have seen me, but you don't believe. All that the Father gives me will come to me, and whoever comes to me I will never cast out because I have come down from Heaven, not to do my own will, but the will of him who sent me. His will is that I should lose nothing of all that he has given me. Instead, I must raise it up on the last day. My Father's will is that everyone who looks on the Son and believes in him should have the life of the ages, and I will raise him up on the last day."

This made the Jews grumble about him because he said, "I am the bread that came down from Heaven."

---

[69] Exodus 16:4

They said, "Isn't this Jesus, Joseph's son? Don't we know his mom and dad? How is it that he says, 'I have come down from Heaven'?"

"Stop grumbling to each other," Jesus interrupted. "No one can come to me unless the Father who sent me draws him. Then I will raise him up on the last day. It's written in the Prophets: [70]*They will all be taught by God.*

Everyone who has heard the Father and learned from Him comes to me. I don't mean that anyone has seen the Father. Only the one who is from God has seen the Father. The truth is – whoever believes has the life of the ages.

I am the bread of life. Your fathers died even though they ate the manna in the wilderness. But this is the bread that comes down from Heaven; anyone may eat of it and not die. I am the living bread that came down from Heaven. If anyone eats of this bread, he will live forever. The bread I will give that the world may live is my flesh."

The Jews started arguing, "How can this man give us his flesh to eat?"

Jesus said, "The truth is – unless you eat the flesh of the Son of Man and drink his blood, you have no life in you. Whoever eats my flesh and drinks my blood has the life of the ages, and I will raise him up on the last day. My flesh is true food and my blood is true drink. Whoever feeds on my flesh and drinks my blood abides in me and I in him. Just as the living Father sent me and I live because of the Father, whoever consumes me will also live because of me. This is the bread that came down from Heaven. It's not like what the fathers ate and yet died; whoever eats this bread will live forever." Jesus said all these things in the synagogue as he taught at Capernaum.

When many of his disciples heard it, they replied, "What you're saying is hard to take in. Who can truly accept it?"

---

[70] Isaiah 54:13

Jesus knew inside that his disciples were complaining about this, and he said, "Does this really offend you? What if you were to see the Son of Man ascending to where he was before? It's the Spirit who gives life; the flesh can do nothing for you. My words to you are spirit and life, but some of you still don't believe." (Jesus knew from the start who didn't believe and who would betray him.) Then he said, "This is why I told you that no one can come to me unless the Father grants it to him."

After this, many of his disciples turned back and didn't walk with him anymore. Jesus asked The Twelve, "Do you want to leave me as well?"

"Who could we go to Lord?" said Peter, "You have the words of life for the ages, and we have believed. Since then, we have come to know that you are the Holy One of God."

"Did I not choose the twelve of you?" Jesus answered. "Yet one of you is a devil." (He was speaking about Judas, Simon Iscariot's son. Judas was one of The Twelve, and he was going to betray Jesus.)

[71]As the Pharisees were gathered around him, along with some of the scribes who had come from Jerusalem, they noticed that some of his disciples' hands were defiled when they ate. (That means they didn't wash their hands before dinner. The Pharisees and all the Jews don't eat without first washing their hands. When they came from the marketplace they were supposed to wash before eating; this upheld the tradition of the elders. Also, there are many other traditions such as the washing of cups, pots, copper vessels, and couches.)

The Pharisees and scribes asked Jesus, "Why don't your disciples obey the tradition of the elders and wash their hands when they eat? Instead, they eat with defiled hands."

Jesus responded with a question, "And why do you break the commandment of God to obey your tradition? You have

---

[71]Mark 7:1-23; Matthew 15:1-20

fully developed your rejection of God's commandment so you can keep your tradition! Moses – as God commanded – said, [72]*Honor your father and your mother,* and, *Whoever speaks evil of his mother or father let him die the death.* But you say that if a man tells his father or his mother, 'Whatever you would've gained from me is Corban,' that is, given to God, then you no longer let him do anything for his parents. For the sake of your tradition you've handed down, you replaced the word of God – and you do this often. You hypocrites! Isaiah was right when he prophesied about you, saying:

[73]*This people honors me with their lips,*
but their heart is far from me;
they worship me in vain,
teaching the commandments of men as doctrines.

"You leave God's commandment and hold onto man's tradition."

Then he called the people to him and said, "All of you listen to me. You need to understand this:

There is nothing outside a person that can defile him by going into his mouth. But the things that come out of a person's mouth are what defile him."

After this, Jesus had left the people and entered the house. The disciples came and asked him, "You do know that the Pharisees were offended when they heard you say this?"

He answered, "Every plant that my heavenly Father has not planted will be rooted up. Leave them alone. They are blind guides, and if the blind lead the blind, they'll both fall into a pit."

"Well explain the parable to us," Peter asked.

"You still don't get it?" Jesus asked. "Don't you see that whatever goes into the mouth passes through the stomach and is eliminated? It cannot defile him because it only enters

---

[72] Exodus 20:12; Deuteronomy 5:16;
    Exodus 21:17; Leviticus 20:9
[73] Isaiah 29:13

his stomach, not his heart. On the other hand, what comes out of the mouth comes from the heart, and this defiles a person." (In saying this he declared that all foods are clean.) He continued, "It's the stuff coming from inside a man, coming out of his heart, things like evil thoughts, sexual immorality, theft, murder, adultery, coveting, wickedness, false witness, deceit, sensuality, envy, slander, pride, and foolishness that defile him. All these evil things come from within, but to eat without washing your hands doesn't hurt anybody."

[74]Jesus got up and left and withdrew to the regions of Tyre and Sidon. He entered a house there and didn't want anyone to know, but he couldn't remain hidden. In no time, a local woman whose little daughter was possessed by a demon heard about him. She came crying, "Have mercy on me, O Lord, Son of David, my daughter is tormented by a demon." But he didn't answer her at all.

The woman was a Gentile, born a Syrophoenician, a Canaanite. Still she begged and pleaded with him to cast the demon out of her daughter.

His disciples came and urged him, "Get rid of her, she won't stop begging us."

"I was only sent to help the lost sheep of the house of Israel," Jesus told them.

Then she came and fell down at his feet, kneeling before him, repeating, "Lord, help me."

"Let the children be fed first," he said. "It's not right to take the children's bread and throw it to the dogs."

"Yes, Lord," she agreed, "but even the dogs under the table eat the children's crumbs that fall from their masters' table."

Jesus marveled, "Woman, your faith is remarkable! It's done! With talk like that, you can go on home; the demon has left your daughter just as you wish." Her daughter was healed

---

[74]Mark 7:24-30; Matthew 15:21-28

73

instantly. She went home and found the child lying in bed. The demon was gone.

[75]He left the region of Tyre and went through Sidon and the Decapolis to the Sea of Galilee. Once there, he walked beside the sea and then up on the mountain and sat down. Huge crowds came to him there, bringing the lame, the blind, the crippled, the mute, and many others. They placed them at his feet, and he healed them.

They also brought a man who was deaf and had a speech impediment, and they begged Jesus to lay his hand on him. Jesus decided to take him aside privately. First, he put his fingers into the man's ears, and then he spit and touched the man's tongue. Next, as he looked up to Heaven, he sighed and said, "Ephphatha," which means, "Open up now." His ears were opened, his tongue was freed, and he started speaking plainly. Jesus told those around not to tell anyone, but the more he tried to hush them, the more they spread it. They were astounded when they saw the mute speaking, the crippled healthy, the lame walking, and the blind seeing. They kept saying, "He does everything right! He even makes the deaf hear and the mute speak." And they went on glorifying the God of Israel.

It was during those days that another big crowd had gathered, and they had nothing to eat. Jesus met with his disciples and said, "My heart goes out to this crowd because they have been with me for three days now and have nothing to eat. I refuse to send them away hungry; some of them have come from far away, and they could even faint on the way home."

His disciples questioned this asking, "What can we do about feeding these people in the middle of nowhere? Where would we get enough bread?"

"How many loaves do you have?" Jesus asked.

"Seven," came the reply.

---

[75]Mark 7:31-8:1-10; Matthew 15:29-39

He directed the crowd to sit down on the ground. He took the seven loaves, gave thanks, and started breaking them and giving them to his disciples to serve to the people. Then someone brought a few small fish. He blessed the fish and told the disciples to distribute those as well. Everyone ate and they were all satisfied.

They gathered up the broken pieces and filled seven baskets with leftovers after fully feeding four thousand men, not counting women and children. Afterward, he sent them away and immediately he got into the boat with his disciples and went to the districts of Dalmanutha and Magadan.

[76]The Pharisees came and began to argue with him, trying to test him by asking for a sign from Heaven. He replied, "When evening comes you say, 'The weather will be good. You can tell by the red sky.' And in the morning you say, 'A storm is coming. Look at that red and threatening sky.' You know how to read the sky, but you can't read the signs of the times."

Jesus sighed deeply from his spirit as he said, "Why does this generation look for a sign? That's what an evil and adulterous generation does. To tell you the truth, no sign will be given except the sign of Jonah." And he left them, got back into the boat, and went to the other side.

Along the way, the disciples realized they had forgotten to bring bread and had only one loaf with them. When they reached the other side, Jesus cautioned them with these words: "Watch out! Beware of the leaven of the Pharisees and Sadducees and the leaven of Herod."

This caused them to enter into a discussion with one another saying, "We didn't bring any bread."

Jesus knew they were talking this way, and he said, "What little faith. Why are you talking about not having bread? You don't get it, do you? You still don't understand. Are your hearts that hard? You have eyes and ears – don't

---

[76]Mark 8:11-26; Matthew 16:1-12

you see and hear with them? Try and remember when I broke the five loaves for the five thousand. How many baskets full of leftovers did you pick up?"

"Twelve," they said.

"How about the seven loaves for the four thousand? How many baskets full of leftovers did you pick up?"

"Seven," they said.

"Do you get it now? How is it you don't understand that I'm not talking about bread? Beware of the leaven of the Pharisees and Sadducees."

Then they understood that he wasn't telling them to beware of the leaven of bread, but of the teaching of the Pharisees and Sadducees.

[77]Later, they came to Bethsaida where some people brought a blind man to Jesus and begged him to touch him. Jesus took the blind man by the hand and led him out of the village. Then he spit on his eyes and laid his hands on him and asked him, "Do you see anything?"

"I see men, but they look like walking trees," he said.

Jesus laid his hands on the man's eyes again, and this time when he opened them, his sight was restored and he saw everything clearly. He sent the man straight home, saying, "Don't even go into the village."

[78]From there, Jesus and his disciples went to the villages of Caesarea Philippi. Along the way, while he was praying alone, he asked his disciples, "Who do people say that the Son of Man is?"

"Some say you are John the Baptizer, and some say Elijah. Others say that Jeremiah or one of the prophets of old has risen."

"But who do you say that I am?"

Simon Peter spoke up saying, "You are the Messiah, the Son of the living God." Jesus demanded that they not tell

---

[77]Mark 8:22-26
[78]Mark 8:27-9:1, Matthew 16:13-28, Luke 9:18-27

anyone about him, and he spoke the following words to Peter: "Blessed are you, Simon Bar-Jonah, for no human revealed this to you. Instead, it was my Father in Heaven. I say you are Peter, and I will build my church on this rock, and the gates of Hell won't stand against it.

I will give you the keys to the kingdom of Heaven, and whatever you bind on Earth will be bound in Heaven, and whatever you loose on Earth will be loosed in Heaven." Once more, he gave strict instructions for the disciples not to tell anyone that he was the Christ.

Jesus began to explain to them saying, "The Son of Man must suffer many things and be rejected by the elders and chief priests and scribes. He must be killed and be raised on the third day." He said it just that plainly.

Peter heard this and took him aside and began to rebuke Jesus saying, "God have mercy! Lord, this will never happen to you!"

Jesus turned to see his disciples and he rebuked Peter saying, "Get out of my way Satan! You're a stumbling block because you're not interested in the things of God, only in the things of man."

And he gathered the crowd and his disciples and said to them, "If anyone wants to follow me, let him deny himself and pick up his cross every day and follow me. Whoever wants to save his life must lose it, but whoever loses his life for my sake and for the gospel, will find and save it. What does it profit a man to gain the whole world and lose his soul? Or what will a man give in exchange for his soul? For the Son of Man is going to return with his angels and pay back each person based on what he's done, and whoever is ashamed of me and my words in this adulterous and sinful generation, the Son of Man will be ashamed of him when he comes in all the glory of himself, his Father, and the holy angels. You should know this truth: some of you standing here won't die until you see the Son of Man coming in his kingdom with power."

[79]After six or eight days, Jesus took only Peter and the brothers (James and John) to pray on top of a high mountain. As he was praying, he was transfigured in front of them, and the appearance of his face was changed so that it was shining like the sun. His clothes became as brilliant as light, dazzling whiter than anyone on Earth could bleach them. Elijah and Moses gloriously appeared to them, and talked with Jesus about his leaving, which he was about to accomplish at Jerusalem.

Now Peter and the others were extremely sleepy, but when they finally woke up, they saw his glory and they saw the two men who stood with him. When the men were leaving, Peter said, "Master, Lord, it is good that we are here. Rabbi, if you want us to, we could make three tents, one for you and one for Moses and one for Elijah" – Peter was so scared he didn't know what he was saying, but while he was still speaking, a bright cloud gathered over them, and they were terrified to be in it. A voice came out of the cloud saying, "This is my beloved Son, my Chosen One, with whom I am well pleased. Listen to him!"

When the disciples heard this, they fell on their faces in terror, but Jesus came and touched them, saying, "Get up, and don't be afraid." When they looked up, only Jesus was there.

As they were coming down the mountain, he told them, "Don't tell anyone the vision until the Son of Man is raised from the dead."

And they kept it among themselves in those days, questioning what this 'rising from the dead' might mean. They also asked Jesus, "Why do the scribes say that Elijah must come first?"

"Elijah does come first to restore all things," he answered. "But Elijah has already come and they didn't recognize him. They treated him like they wanted to, just as

---

[79]Mark 9:2-13; Matthew 17:1-13; Luke 9:28-36

it's written. And you can be sure that the Son of Man will suffer much at their hands and be treated horribly. How can that be?"

Then the disciples understood that he was talking about John the Baptizer.

[80]The next day, when they came down from the mountain, they saw a huge crowd around the disciples and the scribes, who were arguing with one another. As soon as the whole crowd saw Jesus, they were incredibly amazed and ran and greeted him. He asked the disciples, "What are you arguing with them about?"

A man from the crowd came kneeling before him, crying out, "Teacher, please look at my son; have mercy on my only child! He's an epileptic and he suffers so much. Often, it's like he falls into the fire and then into the water. He has a spirit that makes him mute. Whenever it overpowers him, he screams and it throws him down, making him convulse and foam at the mouth. He also grinds his teeth and becomes stiff. It's breaking him and won't leave him alone. I begged your disciples to cast it out, but they couldn't do it."

Jesus answered, "Faithless and twisted generation, how long will I be with you? How long will I endure you? Bring him to me."

They brought the boy, and when the spirit saw him, immediately it convulsed and threw the boy to the ground and he rolled around, foaming at the mouth. "How long has this been happening to him?" Jesus asked his dad.

"Since he was a child. It's like it just throws him into fire and into water trying to destroy him. If you can do anything, show some compassion and help us."

"'If you can?'" said Jesus. "Anything is possible for believers!"

As soon as the words were out of Jesus' mouth, the father cried out, "I believe, help my unbelief!"

---

[80]Mark 9:14-32; Matthew 17:14-23; Luke 9:37-45

Jesus saw a crowd running toward them, and he rebuked the demon saying, "You deaf and dumb spirit, I command you to come out of him and never enter him again."

There was a loud cry, and the demon threw him down again, convulsing violently. But it came out, leaving the boy like a corpse, so that most of them said, "He's dead." Jesus took him by the hand and helped him up, and he was instantly healed. Jesus gave him back to his father, and they were all astonished at the majesty of God. As they went inside the house, his disciples asked him privately, "Why couldn't we cast it out?"

"Because your faith is too small," he replied, "and the only way to drive this kind out is by prayer. The truth is – if you have faith like a grain of mustard seed, you can say to this mountain, 'Move over,' and it will move, and nothing will be impossible for you."

Marveling at all he was doing, they left there and journeyed through Galilee, but he didn't want anyone to know because he was teaching his disciples and telling them, "Let this sink in: the Son of Man is going to be delivered into the hands of men, and they will kill him. When he is dead, three days later he will rise." Yet, they didn't understand this. It was hidden from them, and they were so troubled they were afraid to ask him about it.

[81]After this, Jesus traveled around Galilee, but not Judea because the Jews were waiting to kill him. It was time for the Jewish Feast of Booths, and his brothers said to him, "No one works secretly if he seeks to be known openly. Leave here and go to Judea. Then your disciples there may see your works. Since you are doing these things, reveal it all to the world." Although his brothers said this, they still didn't believe in him.

"It's not time for me," Jesus answered, "but it's always the right time for you. The world cannot hate you, but it

---

[81]John 7:1-9

hates me because I talk about it and how its works are evil. You go to the feast. I'm not going to this one because my time has not yet fully come." He said this and stayed in Galilee."

[82]After his brothers had gone to the feast, he went also, but in secret. The Jews were looking for him there, saying, "Where is he?" As the people whispered, some said, "He is a good man," while others said, "He is deceiving the people."

No one spoke openly about him for fear of the Jews.

During the middle of the feast, Jesus went into the temple and began teaching while the Jews marveled, "How can this man know all these things when he has never studied?"

"My teaching doesn't belong to me," Jesus answered, "but to him who sent me. If a person's will is to do God's will, then he'll know whether my teaching is from God or if I speak on my own. The one who speaks on his own authority does it for the praise of others, but a true person seeks the glory of the one who sent him, and there is nothing false in him. Didn't Moses give you the Law? Yet none of you keeps it. So why do you want to kill me?"

The crowd yelled, "YOU HAVE A DEMON WHO IS TRYING TO KILL YOU!"

"I did one thing," Jesus said, "and you're all amazed. Moses gave you circumcision (which was really from the fathers) and you circumcise a man on the Sabbath. If a man receives circumcision on the Sabbath so he won't break the Law of Moses, then why are you mad at me because I made a man's whole body well on the Sabbath? Stop judging on appearances. Instead, judge with right judgment."

Some of those from Jerusalem reasoned, "Aren't they trying to kill this man? And here he is talking in plain sight while they say nothing! What if the leaders know that this really is the Messiah? The problem is that we know where this

---

[82]John 7:10-53

man comes from, but when the Messiah appears, no one will know where he comes from."

Jesus continued teaching in the temple, saying, "Yes, you do know me, and you know where I come from. But I haven't come on my own. The one who sent me is real, but you don't know him. I know him because I came from him, and he sent me."

They were trying to arrest him, but no one laid a hand on him because his hour had not yet come. Many others believed in him and asked, "When the Messiah appears, will he do more signs than this man has done?"

The Pharisees heard the crowd whispering these things about him, and the chief priests and Pharisees sent officers to arrest him. Jesus said, "I will be with you a little longer, and then I'm going back to the one who sent me. You'll look for me, but you won't find me since you cannot go where I'm going."

The Jews questioned one another: "Where does this man think he can go that we can't find him? Is he planning to go to the Dispersion among the Greeks and teach them? What does he mean when he says, 'You'll look for me and you won't find me,' and, 'You cannot go where I'm going'?"

On the last and most important day of the feast, Jesus stood up and cried out, "If anyone is thirsty, come to me and drink. Whoever believes in me, as the Scripture has said, [83] *Rivers of living water will flow out of his heart.*"

Jesus said this referring to the Spirit that those who believed in him were to receive. Until now, the Spirit had not been given because Jesus was not yet glorified.

Some of the people who heard this said, "This really is the Prophet."

Others said, "This is the Messiah."

---

[83] Isaiah 58:11

But some argued, "Is the Messiah coming from Galilee? Doesn't the Scripture say that the Christ comes from the line of David and from Bethlehem where David is from?"

So the people were divided over him. Some of them wanted to arrest him, but no one laid a hand on him.

Then the officers came to the chief priests and Pharisees, who said, "Why didn't you bring him?"

"We've never heard anyone talk like this man!" the officers answered.

"Have you also been deceived?" the Pharisees replied. "Have any leaders of the Pharisees believed in him? This crowd that does not even know the Law is condemned."

Nicodemus said, "Does our Law judge a man without a trial? Don't we listen to him to find out what he is doing?" (This is the same Nicodemus who went to Jesus earlier and was also a Jewish ruler.)

They replied, "Are you from Galilee too? Study and you will see that no prophet arises from Galilee." Then they all went home, but [84]Jesus went to the Mount of Olives. Early in the morning, he came back to the temple and sat down to teach all the people who came to hear him. The scribes and Pharisees brought a woman who had been caught in adultery. They put her in the middle of everyone and said to him, "Teacher, this woman has been caught in the act of adultery. In the Law, Moses commanded us to stone women like this. What do you say?"

They were doing this to test Jesus so they could charge him with breaking the Law. Jesus bent down and began to write on the ground with his finger, while they kept asking him the question. Then he straightened up and said, "Let the person who has no sin throw the first stone at her." He stooped down again and continued writing on the ground. They all heard him, and the older ones started leaving first, one by one, until Jesus was left alone with the woman

---

[84]John 8:1-11

standing there. "Woman, where are they?" Jesus said as he stood up. "Has no one condemned you?"

"No one, Lord," she said.

"I don't condemn you either. You can go, but from now on, don't sin anymore."

[85]Jesus spoke to those who had come, saying, "I am the light of the world. Whoever follows me will not walk in darkness but will have the light of life."

And the Pharisees reacted, "You are being your own witness for yourself, and your testimony is a lie."

"Even if I do bear witness about myself, my testimony is true," Jesus responded. "For I know where I came from and where I'm going. But you don't – you judge according to the flesh. I don't judge anybody, and even if I do, my judgment is true because I don't judge alone, but with the Father who sent me. In your Law it's written that the testimony of two men is true. I bear witness about myself, and so does the Father who sent me."

"Where is your Father?" they inquired.

"You don't know me or my Father. If you knew me, you would also know my Father." He said all this while teaching in the temple room where they kept the offerings, but no one arrested him because his hour had not yet come.

He continued, "I'm leaving, and you will search for me, and you will die in your sin. Where I'm going, you cannot come."

This made the Jews say, "Is he going to commit suicide since he says, 'Where I'm going, you cannot come'?"

He said to them, "You're from down here; I'm from up there. You're part of this world, I'm not. I told you that you would die in your sins, and you will unless you believe that I am."

"Who are you?" they asked.

---

[85]John 8:12-59

"Just what I have been telling you from the beginning. I have so much to say to you and so much to judge, and I tell the world what he tells me. He sent me, and he is the truth."

They didn't understand that he had been talking about the Father. Jesus said, "When you have lifted up the Son of Man, then you will know that I am, and that I don't do anything on my own, but I say only what the Father taught me. He sent me, and he is with me. He hasn't left me alone because I always do the things that please him."

Many believed in him as he said all this, and Jesus told the Jews who had believed, "You really are my disciples if you live in my word, and you will know the truth, and the truth will set you free."

Others answered, "We are Abraham's descendants and have never been enslaved to anyone! How dare you say, 'You will become free.'"

Jesus answered them, "The truth is – everyone who sins is a slave to sin. The slave does not stay in the house forever, but the son does. So if the Son sets you free, your freedom will be real. I know that you're Abraham's descendants, yet you're trying to kill me because my word has no place in you. I talk about what I've seen with my Father, and you do what your father tells you to do."

"Abraham is our father," they retorted.

"If you were Abraham's children," said Jesus, "you would be doing what Abraham did, but now you seek to kill me – a man who told you the truth that I heard from God. This is not what Abraham did. You're doing what your father did."

They said, "We were not born of sexual immorality. We have one Father – that's God."

Jesus said to them, "If God were your Father, you would love me because I came from God and I'm here. I didn't come on my own, but he sent me. Why don't you understand what I tell you? It's because you can't stand to hear my word. Your father is the Devil, and you want to do your father's lusts. He was a murderer from the beginning and has nothing to do with the truth because there is no truth in him. When he lies, it comes out of his own character, for he is a liar and the father of lies. You don't believe me because I tell the truth. Which one of you can show me my sin? If I tell the truth, why don't you believe me? Whoever belongs to God listens to his words. The reason you don't hear them – you don't belong to God."

The Jews demanded, "Are we not right in saying that you are a demon-possessed Samaritan?"

"I don't have a demon, but I honor my Father, and you dishonor me," Jesus answered. "Still, I don't seek my own glory, but there is one who does, and he is the judge. The truth is – no one will ever die who keeps my word."

"Now we know you're demon-possessed!" they said. "Abraham died and so did the prophets, but you say, 'If anyone keeps my word, he will never die.' Are you greater than our father Abraham? He and the prophets have all died! Who do you think you are?"

Jesus answered, "If I glorify myself, then I have no glory. It's my Father who glorifies me. You say, 'He is our God,' but you haven't known him. I know him; if I said I didn't, I would be a liar like you. But I do know him, and I obey his word. Your father Abraham rejoiced that he would see my day, and he was glad when he did."

The Jews asked, "Have you seen Abraham, although you're not even fifty years old?"

"To tell you the truth, before Abraham was, I am," said Jesus.

That's when they picked up stones to throw at him, but Jesus hid and left the temple.

[86]As he passed by, Jesus saw a man who had been born blind. His disciples wondered, "Rabbi, whose sin caused this man to be born blind? Was it his or his parents'?"

---

[86]John 9:1-41

"Neither," said Jesus. "It happened in order that God's works might be revealed in him. We must do the works of him who sent me while it is day; night is coming and no one can work then. As long as I'm in the world, I am the light of the world."

After he said this, he spit on the ground and made mud with the saliva. He smeared the mud on the man's eyes and told him, "Go wash in the pool of Siloam" (Siloam means Sent). The man went and washed and came back seeing.

The neighbors and those who knew him as a beggar were saying, "Isn't this the man who used to sit and beg?"

"That's him," some said, while others said, "No, it just looks like him."

The whole time the man was saying, "Yes, it's me."

"How were your eyes opened?" they asked.

"The man named Jesus made mud and put it on my eyes and told me, 'Go to Siloam and wash.' I did and then I could see."

They said, "Where is he?"

"I don't know."

They brought him to the Pharisees who discovered that Jesus had done this on a Sabbath day. So the Pharisees asked him again how he had received his sight. The man answered, "He put mud on my eyes, and I washed, and then I could see."

The Pharisees were divided between those who said, "This man did not keep the Sabbath because he is not from God!" and others who said, "How can a sinner do signs like this?"

And they asked the blind man, "What do you say about him since he opened your eyes?"

"I say he's a prophet."

The Jews did not believe that he had been blind and then healed until they called the man's parents and asked them, "Is this your son who you say was born blind? How does he see now?"

His parents answered, "This is our son, and he was born blind, but we don't know how he can see now, nor do we know who opened his eyes. Ask him. He's old enough to speak for himself." (His parents answered this way because they were afraid of the Jews since they knew the Jews had already put the word out that if anyone confessed Jesus to be the Messiah, he would be kicked out of the synagogue.) That's why they said, "He's old enough, ask him."

So they called the man who had been blind a second time and said, "Give God the praise. We know this man is a sinner."

He answered, "I don't know whether he's a sinner or not. I do know one thing – I was blind and now I can see."

They asked him, "What did he do to you? How did he open your eyes?"

"I told you already, and you wouldn't listen," he said. "Why do you want to hear it again? Do you want to become his disciples too?"

They began to lash out at him, saying, "You're his disciple, but we are disciples of Moses! We know that God talked to Moses, but as for this man, we don't even know where he comes from!"

"Well that is amazing! You don't know where he comes from, but he opened my eyes, and we know that God won't listen to sinners. On the other hand, God listens to anyone who worships him and does his will. Since the world began, no one has ever heard of anyone opening the eyes of a man born blind. This man couldn't do anything unless he was from God."

As they threw him out, they said, "You were born totally in sin, and now you think you can teach us?"

Jesus heard that they threw him out, and he went and found the man and asked him, "Do you believe in the Son of Man?"

"Who is he sir, so that I can believe in him?"

"You've seen him before, and now he's talking to you."

"Lord, I believe," he declared as he worshiped him.

Then Jesus said, "I came into this world to judge, so the blind could see and the seeing could become blind."

Some of the Pharisees nearby heard these things and said, "Are we blind too?"

"If you were blind, you wouldn't be guilty. But since you say, 'We see,' your guilt is on you."

[87]"The truth is – the man who enters the sheepfold by climbing in rather than using the door is a thief and a robber. The real shepherd of the sheep uses the door, and the gatekeepers open it for him. His sheep hear his voice as he calls them by name and leads them. Once all of his own sheep have come out, then he goes before them, and they follow him because they know his voice. They will not follow a stranger. They will run away, for they don't know a stranger's voice." Jesus used this metaphor, but they did not understand what he was saying.

So Jesus said, "The truth is – I am the door of the sheep. All who came before me are thieves and robbers, but the sheep did not listen to them. I am the door. If anyone comes in by me, he will be safe and will come and go and find pasture."

"The thief comes only to steal and kill and destroy. I came that they may have life – life to its fullest. I am the good shepherd. The good shepherd lays down his life for the sheep. The man only hired to do a job – not the real shepherd who owns the sheep – will leave them when he sees the wolf coming and run away as the wolf catches and scatters the sheep. He runs away because it's just a job – he doesn't care about the sheep. I am the good shepherd. I know my own and my own know me – the same way the Father knows me and I know the Father. I lay down my life for the sheep. I have other sheep that are not of this fold, and I'll bring them in as well, and they will listen to my voice. There will be one flock and one shepherd. That's why the

---

[87]John 10:1-21

Father loves me because I lay down my life so that I may take it up again. No one takes my life from me – I choose to lay it down. I have the power to lay it down, and I have the power to take it up. This is a commandment I received from my Father."

Once again, the Jews were divided over Jesus' message. Some said, "Why are we listening to him? He is demon-possessed and insane."

Others argued, "Demon-possessed people don't talk like this. Can a demon open blind eyes?"

[88]It was around this time that the Feast of Dedication took place in Jerusalem. It was winter and Jesus was walking in the temple in Solomon's colonnade. The Jews gathered around him asking, "How long will you keep us in suspense? If you are the Messiah, say it plainly."

"I did, but you don't believe. The works I do in my Father's name witness about me, but you don't believe because you are not part of my flock. My sheep hear my voice, and I know them, and they follow me. I give them life for the age. They will never die, and no one will snatch them out of my hand. My Father, who has given them to me, is greater than all, and no one is able to snatch them out of the Father's hand. The Father and I are one."

As the Jews picked up rocks again to stone Jesus, he asked them, "I have shown you many good works from the Father; which ones am I being stoned for?"

"We are not stoning you for good works. We are stoning you for blasphemy – You're a man making yourself out to be God!"

"Isn't [89]*I said you are gods'* written in your Law?" Jesus asked. "If he called them gods to whom the word of God came – and the Scripture can't be broken – then how do you say, 'You are blaspheming' to the one the Father consecrated

---

[88]John 10:22-39
[89] Psalm 82:6

and sent into the world because I said, 'I am the Son of God'? If I am not doing my Father's works, then don't believe me. But if I do the Father's works, even though you don't believe me, believe the works so you can know and understand that the Father is in me and I am in the Father." And they tried to arrest him again, but he escaped.

+++

[90]When they arrived in Capernaum, the collectors of the half-shekel tax approached Peter and asked, "Does your teacher pay the tax or not?"

"Yes," answered Peter.

Once they were in the house, Jesus brought it up first, saying, "Simon, what do you think? Who do the kings of the earth take taxes and tolls from, their sons or others?"

When Peter answered, "From others," Jesus replied, "Then the sons don't have to pay. However, so we don't offend them, go to the sea and cast a line. Take the first fish you catch, and when you open its mouth you'll find a shekel. Take that shekel and give it to them for me and you."

While they were still in the house, he sat down and asked The Twelve, "What were you discussing on the way here?" But nobody said a word because on the way they had argued about who was the greatest. Finally they asked him, "Who is the greatest in the kingdom of Heaven?"

He answered, "If anyone wants to be first, he must be in last place and be everyone's servant."

He knew how they were reasoning this out in their hearts, so he called a child and put him in the middle of them. He picked the child up in his arms and said, "Whoever accepts a child like this in my name accepts me, and whoever accepts me is not accepting me but the one who sent me. The truth is – unless you change and become like children, you'll

---

[90]Mark 9:33-50; Matthew 17:24-18:35; Luke 9:46-50

never enter the kingdom of Heaven. But whoever humbles himself like this child is the greatest in the kingdom of Heaven, for the one who is least among you all is the one who is great."

John said to him, "Teacher, we saw someone casting out demons in your name, and we tried to stop him because he was not following us."

"Don't stop him," said Jesus, "because no one will be able to talk bad about me right after he does a mighty work in my name. Whoever is not against us is for us. Truly, whoever gives you a cup of water to drink because you belong to Christ certainly won't lose his reward."

He continued, "Whoever receives one child like this in my name receives me, but whoever causes one of these little ones who believes in me to sin, it would be better for him to have a big millstone strapped around his neck and drown in the deepest sea."

"Woe to the world for tempting people to sin! It's necessary that temptations come, but woe to the one who brings it! If your hand or your foot causes you to sin, cut it off and throw it away. It's better for you to go into life crippled or lame than with two hands or two feet to be thrown into Hell, the unquenchable fire of the ages. And if your eye causes you to sin, tear it out and throw it away. If you go into life and God's kingdom with one eye instead of two, that's better than being thrown into the fires of Hell, 'where the worm does not die and the fire is not quenched.' Everyone will be salted with fire, and salt is a good thing, but if the salt has lost its saltiness, how will you make it salty again? I want you to be salty and at peace with one another, making sure that you don't despise one of these little ones. I'm telling you, their heavenly angels always see my Father's face in Heaven."

"What do you think about this? If a man has a hundred sheep and one of them wanders off, won't he leave the ninety-nine on the mountains and go search for the one that left? And the truth is – if he finds it, he rejoices more over it than over the ninety-nine that never went astray. My Father in Heaven does not want a single one of these little ones to die."

He taught them this as well: "If your brother sins against you, go tell him in private – just the two of you. If he listens, you won your brother back. But if he will not listen, go back to him with one or two others. That way, [91]*what you accuse him of can be founded on the evidence of two or three witnesses.* If he refuses to listen to them, tell it to the church. If he will not listen even to the church, you should relate to him as if he were a Gentile or a tax collector. The truth is –whatever you bind on Earth will be bound in Heaven, and whatever you loose on Earth will be loosed in Heaven. Let me repeat this. If two or three gather in my name on Earth and agree to ask for anything, my Father in Heaven will do it for them, and I will stand with them.

Peter came closer and asked, "Lord, how many times do I forgive my brother when he sins against me? Would seven be the limit?"

"No, not seven times, but seventy times seven. I'll tell you what it's like. You can compare the kingdom of Heaven to a king who decided to settle accounts with his servants. As he was doing this, one servant was brought to him who owed him ten million dollars. Since he couldn't pay, his master decided to sell him, along with his wife and children, and all he had and pay the debt. The servant fell to his knees, begging him, 'Be patient with me, and I will pay it all back.' His master had pity, let him go, and forgave the debt.

That same servant went out and found one of his fellow servants who owed him ten thousand dollars. He grabbed him and started choking him, demanding, 'Pay up what you owe me!' His fellow servant fell down and begged him, 'Be patient with me, and I will pay it all back,' but that servant refused to be patient and had him put in prison until he paid the debt. When the other servants saw what had happened,

---

[91] Deuteronomy 19:15

93

they felt sorry for the imprisoned man and told it all to their master. Then his master called him in and said, 'You wicked servant! I forgave all your debt because you begged me. Don't you think you should have shown the same mercy to others that I showed to you?' His master was very angry and he handed him over to the jailers until he could pay back all his debt. My heavenly Father will do the same to every one of you, if you don't forgive your brother from your heart."

Judea and Jordan

[92]After Jesus had finished saying all these things and it was closer to the time for him to ascend, he left Galilee determined to go to Jerusalem. On the way, he sent messengers ahead who entered a Samaritan village to make preparations for him, but the people there didn't receive him because he was headed for Jerusalem. His disciples, James and John, saw this and fumed, "Lord, do you want us to call down fire from Heaven and destroy them?" Jesus turned and rebuked them as he continued on to another village toward Jerusalem.

As they were traveling, they passed between Samaria and Galilee. When he entered a village, ten lepers stood at a distance shouting, "Jesus! Master, have mercy on us!"

"Go and show yourselves to the priests," Jesus shouted back when he saw them. So they headed that way and were healed before they got to the priest. One of them, realizing he was healed, returned, praising God with a loud voice. He fell on his face at Jesus' feet, thanking him.

Since he was a Samaritan, Jesus wondered, "Ten were healed, right? Where are the other nine? Has nobody but this foreigner wanted to come back and praise God?" He told the man, "Get up, you're ready to go – your faith has made you well."

He traveled on to the region of Judea and beyond the Jordan where John began immersing people. He healed the crowds that gathered there and taught them as he usually did. Many came to him believing and saying, "John didn't do miracles, but everything John said about this man was right."

---

[92]Mark 10:1; Matthew 19:1-2;
Luke 9:51-56, 10:1-20; 17:11-19;
John 10:40-42

After this, the Lord appointed seventy-two others and sent them ahead of him, two by two, into every place where he was about to go. "The harvest is plentiful," he said, "but the workers are few. Pray passionately to the Lord of the harvest to send out workers into his harvest. Keep going. I'm sending you out as lambs among the wolves. Don't carry a wallet, backpack, or sandals, and don't stop to socialize along the way. When you enter a house, first say, 'Shalom (peace) on this house!' If a son of peace is there, your peace will rest on him. If not, your shalom will return to you. I want you to stay in the same house, eating and drinking what they provide because workers deserve their pay. Don't go from house to house. Whenever you come into town and they receive you, eat what they give you and heal the sick there and say, 'The kingdom of God has come close to you.' But if you come to a town and they don't receive you, walk out in its streets and say, 'The dust of your town that clings to our feet – we wipe off against you. Still, we want you to know that the kingdom of God has come close to you.' I tell you, when The Day comes, it will be more bearable for Sodom than for that town."

"Woe to you, Chorazin! Woe to you, Bethsaida! If the miracles done in you had been done in Tyre and Sidon, they would have repented a long time ago, sitting in sackcloth and ashes. That's why it will be more bearable in the judgment for Tyre and Sidon than for you. As for Capernaum, do you think you're going to Heaven? You're going to Hell!"

"The one who hears you, hears me, and the one who rejects you, rejects me, and the one who rejects me, rejects him who sent me."

Later, the seventy-two came back celebrating, "Lord, even the demons obey us in your name!"

Jesus replied, "I saw Satan fall from Heaven like lightning. Yes, I've given you authority to walk on snakes and scorpions; your power trumps the power of the enemy, and nothing will hurt you. Even so, don't get excited that the spirits are subject to you, but be excited that your names are written in Heaven."

[93]In that same hour he rejoiced in the Holy Spirit and said, "I thank you, Father, Lord of Heaven and Earth, that you have hidden these things from the wise and understanding and have revealed them to little children. Yes, Father, that's your gracious will.

My Father handed all things over to me, and no one knows the Son except the Father, and no one knows the Father except the Son and anyone to whom the Son chooses to reveal him."

"All of you who are burdened down and working so hard, come to me and I will give you rest. Yoke yourself to me and learn from me, for I am gentle and down-to-earth. Then you will find rest for your souls because my yoke is easy and my burden is light."

Then he spoke privately to the disciples, saying, "How blessed are the eyes that see what you are seeing. For many prophets and kings longed to see and hear what you have, but they never did."

Then a lawyer stood up and tested him. He said, "Teacher, what do I have to do to inherit the life of the ages?"

"What's written in the Law?" asked Jesus.

[94]*"You shall love the Lord your God with all your heart, with all your soul, with all your strength, and with all your mind, and you shall love your neighbor as yourself,"* said the lawyer.

"That's right. If you do that, you will live," agreed Jesus.

But he wanted to make himself out to be righteous, so he asked Jesus, "And who is my neighbor?"

Jesus answered him, "There was a certain man who went down to Jericho where thieves attacked him. They stripped him and beat him and left him there nearly dead. Later, it

---

[93]Luke 10:21-37; Matthew 11:25-30
[94] Deuteronomy 6:5; Leviticus 11:18

happened that a certain priest was passing by that way, and when he saw him he moved to the other side of the road to avoid him. In the same way, a Levite came and looked at him, but also crossed over to avoid him. Then a certain Samaritan was traveling and came upon the man. When he saw him, he felt compassion and bandaged up his wounds using oil and wine. He put the man on his own animal and brought him to an inn and took care of him.

The next day, he gave two days wages to the innkeeper and said, 'Take care of this man, and I will repay you for any extra costs when I come back.' Now which of these three, do you think, proved to be a neighbor to the man who was attacked by robbers?"

"The one who showed him mercy," he said.

"Then you go do the same thing."

[95]As they traveled on, Jesus came into a village where a woman named Martha welcomed him into her house. She had a sister named Mary who sat at the Lord's feet and listened to his teaching, but Martha was too busy serving. She went to him and said, "Lord, don't you care that my sister has left me to do all the serving? Tell her to help me."

"Martha, Martha," answered Jesus, "you are stressed over many things, but only one thing is necessary. Mary chose the good, and you can't take that away from her."

Later, Jesus was praying somewhere, and when he finished, one of his disciples said to him, "Lord, teach us to pray like John taught his disciples."

Jesus said, "When you pray, say,
"Father, hallowed be your name,
your kingdom come.
Give us bread for the day
and forgive us for our sins,
and we will forgive everyone who sins against us.
And do not lead us into temptation."

---

[95]Luke 10:38-42, 11:1-13

He also said, "You have a friend and you go to him at midnight saying, 'Friend, let me borrow three loaves of bread because another friend of mine has dropped by and I don't have anything to feed him.' And he responds without even opening the door, 'Don't bother me. I've already locked up for the night and my children and I are in bed. I can't get up and give you anything.' I tell you what will happen, although he won't get up and give him anything because he's his friend, yet because of his friend's persistence he will get up and give him whatever he needs. So I say, ask, and it will be given to you; seek, and you will find; knock, and it will be opened to you. Because everyone who asks, receives, and the one who seeks, finds, and to the one who knocks, it will be opened."

"Which one of you fathers, if his son asks for a fish, will give him a snake instead, or if he asks for an egg, will give him a scorpion? If you then, who are evil, know how to give good gifts to your children, how much more will the heavenly Father give the Holy Spirit to those who ask him!"

[96]While Jesus was speaking, a Pharisee asked him to come to his home for dinner. Jesus went to his house and reclined at the table. The Pharisee couldn't believe that he did not wash up before dinner. Then the Lord said to him, "You Pharisees clean the outside of the cup and dish, but inside you are full of greed and wickedness. You fools! Didn't the one who made the outside make the inside also? But if you give away what is inside you, notice – everything is clean for you.

"Woe to you Pharisees! You're careful to tithe, giving ten percent of mint and rue and every herb, but you neglect justice and the love of God. You should have tithed each of these without neglecting anything else.

Woe to you Pharisees! Because you love the best seats in the synagogues and how you are greeted in town. Woe to

---

[96]Luke 11:37-53

you! For you are like unmarked graves, and people walk over them without knowing it."

One of the lawyers spoke up, "Teacher, you are insulting us as well when you talk like this."

"Woe to you lawyers also! You load people with heavy burdens, but you won't lift a finger to help carry them. Woe to you! You dig the graves of the prophets whom your fathers killed. You are not only witnesses, you also approve your fathers' deeds – they killed them and you dug the hole. This is why God in his wisdom said, 'I will send them prophets and apostles, and they will kill and persecute some of them,' so that the blood of all the prophets, shed since the world began, may be charged against this generation, from Abel's to Zechariah's murder – all of them who perished between the altar and the sanctuary. Yes, this generation will be held responsible. Woe to you lawyers! For you have taken away the key of knowledge. You didn't go in yourselves, and you hindered those who were entering."

As he left there, the scribes and the Pharisees began to pressure and provoke him to talk about many different subjects, waiting to trap him in something he might say.

[97]In the meantime, when so many thousands of people had crowded together that they were trampling one another, he began to say to his disciples first, "Beware of the leaven of the Pharisees, which is hypocrisy. Nothing is covered up that will not be revealed or hidden that will not be known. Whatever you've said in the dark will be heard in the light, and what you've whispered in private will be shouted from the housetops."

"You're my friends, and I'm telling you, don't fear those who kill the body and after that can do nothing more to you. But I will warn you whom to fear – fear him who can both kill you and throw you into Hell. Oh yes, you had better fear him!

---

[97]Luke 12:1-13:9

You can buy five sparrows for two pennies, right? But God will not have forgotten those five sparrows. Beyond that, even the hairs of your head are all numbered. Don't be afraid; you are far more valuable than many sparrows."

"Let me also tell you this, everyone who confesses me before men, the Son of Man will confess before the angels of God. But the one who denies me before men will be denied before the angels of God. And everyone who speaks a word against the Son of Man will be forgiven, but the one who blasphemes against the Holy Spirit will not be forgiven. So when they bring you before the synagogues, rulers, and authorities, don't be nervous about how you are going to defend yourself or what you should say, for in that moment the Holy Spirit will tell you what to say."

Someone in the crowd said to him, "Teacher, tell my brother to divide the inheritance with me."

"Man, who made me a judge or mediator over you?" Jesus answered. Then he said, "Be careful and guard yourself against all coveting because your life is not in how much stuff you have."

He also told this parable: "A rich man had some land that grew a lot of food, and he thought to himself, 'What am I going to do? I have nowhere to store my crops. I know what I'll do. I will tear down my barns and build bigger ones to store it all. Then I'll say to my soul, "Soul, you have plenty stored up for many years. Relax, eat, drink, and be merry." But God said to him, 'You fool! Tonight your soul is required of you. Now who will get all that you worked for?'" Jesus remarked, "This is how it is for the one who lays up treasure for himself and is not rich toward God."

And he told his disciples, "Therefore I tell you, don't worry about your life or your body by asking what you will eat or what you will wear. For life is about more than food, and the body is about more than clothing. Think about the ravens; they don't sow or reap, they don't have storehouses or barns, and yet God feeds them. How much more valuable are you than the birds? Anyway, which of you can add a

101

single hour to your life through anxiety? If you can't do something as small as that, why are you stressed about the rest? Consider the lilies. How do they grow? They don't wear themselves out or spin, but I tell you, not even Solomon in all his glory was clothed like one of these. If God so clothes the grass, which is alive in the field today and tomorrow is thrown into the oven, how much more will he clothe you? O you of little faith! And don't be wrapped up in what you will eat and what you will drink. Stop worrying! All the people of the world scramble after these things, and your Father knows that you need them. Instead, seek his kingdom, and you'll have everything you need."

"Don't be afraid little flock. It makes your Father happy to give you the kingdom. Sell your stuff and give to the needy. Get moneybags that don't grow old, with a treasure in the heavens that will not fail, where no thief can break in and no moth destroys. For where your treasure is, there your heart will be also."

He said, "Stay dressed and ready to go, and keep your lights on. Be like men who are waiting for the master to come home from the wedding feast so they can open the door to him as soon as he knocks. Blessed are those servants the master finds awake when he comes. Truly, he will get dressed to serve and have them recline at the table, and he will be their server. If he comes in the second or third watch and finds them awake, oh how they will be blessed! But know this, if the head of the house had known what time the thief was coming, he would not have left his house to be broken into. That's why you have to be ready – the Son of Man is coming at an unexpected hour."

Peter wondered, "Lord, are you telling this story for us or for everyone?"

The Lord responded, "Who do you think is the faithful and wise manager, the one the master will put in charge over his household to give them all of their food at the right time? Blessed is that servant when his master comes and finds him doing his job. Truly I say to you, he will put him in charge of all he owns. But if that servant says to himself, 'My master won't be here anytime soon,' and begins to beat the servants – even the women – and to eat and drink and get drunk, then the servant's master will come on a day when he is totally unexpected, and will cut him in pieces and put him with the unfaithful. Furthermore, that servant who knew his master's will but did not get ready or do his will, will be beaten severely. But the one who did not know his master's will, and did what deserved a beating, will only receive a light beating. Every person who has been given much will have much required of him, and they will demand all the more from the one to whom they entrusted more."

"I came to throw fire down on the earth, and I wish the fire was already lit! I have a baptism to be immersed with, and I have great distress until it is finished! Do you think I have come to bring peace on Earth? No. I tell you I bring division. From now on, in one house there will be five divided – three against two and two against three. [98]*Father will be divided against son and son against father, mother against daughter and daughter against mother, mother-in-law against her daughter-in-law and daughter-in-law against mother-in-law.*"

He also said to the crowds, "When you see a cloud rising in the west, instantly you say, 'Rain is on the way,' and you're right, it is. When you see the south wind blowing, you say, 'It's going to be a hot one,' and so it is. You hypocrites! You know how to read the earth and sky, why do you not know how to read the times?"

"And why don't you judge what is right for you? As you go with your accuser before the judge, try to settle with him on the way. Otherwise, he may drag you into court where the judge will hand you over to the officer, and the officer will put you in prison. I tell you, you won't ever get out until you have paid the very last penny."

---

[98] Micah 7:6

Some people there at that time told Jesus about the Galileans whose blood Pilate had mixed with their sacrifices. He answered them, "Do you think these Galileans were worse sinners than all the other Galileans based on how they suffered? The answer is 'No.' But unless you repent, you're all going to die. Or what about those eighteen the tower in Siloam fell on and killed? Do you think they were worse sinners than all the others who lived in Jerusalem? No, I tell you, but unless you repent, you will all die as well."

Then he told this parable: "A man had a fig tree planted in his vineyard, and he came looking for fruit on it and found none. He said to the vinedresser, 'I've been looking for fruit on this fig tree for three years now and I never find any. Cut it down. Why should it waste the ground it's planted in?' The man answered him, 'Sir, give it one more year, and let me dig around it and fertilize it. If it bears fruit next year, good, but if not, you can cut it down.'"

[99]He was teaching in one of the synagogues on the Sabbath, and there was a woman who had a crippling spirit for eighteen years. She was bent over and could not stand up straight. When Jesus saw her, he called her over and said, "Woman, you are freed from your disability."

He laid his hands on her, and immediately she could stand up straight, and she glorified God. But the ruler of the synagogue was mad because Jesus had healed on the Sabbath. The ruler said to the people, "There are six days for work to be done. You should come to be healed on those days, not on the Sabbath day."

"You hypocrites!" answered Jesus. "Don't each of you untie your ox or donkey from the manger and lead it to water on the Sabbath? So shouldn't this woman, a daughter of Abraham, whom Satan has bound for eighteen years, be set free from this bondage on the Sabbath day?"

---

[99]Luke 13:10-21

This put his critics to shame, and all the people rejoiced at all the wonderful things he did.

"What can we compare the kingdom of God to, or what story can we use for it? The kingdom of Heaven is like a grain of mustard seed that a man took and planted in his garden, and it grew and became a tree, and the birds came to nest in its shade."

He told them another parable, "What can I compare the kingdom of God to? It's like yeast that a woman took and hid in a bushel of flour until it was all leavened."

[100]After this, he continued on through towns and villages, teaching and journeying toward Jerusalem. Along the way someone asked, "Lord, will only a few people be saved?"

He answered this way: "Strive to get in through the narrow door. I'm telling you that many will try to get in and won't be able to. Once the master of the house gets up and shuts the door, and you come and stand outside and knock on the door, saying, 'Lord, open the door for us,' he will answer you, 'I don't know where you come from.' Then you will say, 'We ate and drank together. You even taught in our streets.' But he will say, 'I'm telling all you evil workers, I do not know where you come from, and I want you to leave and get away from me!' And when you are rejected and sent away, there will be weeping and gnashing of teeth in that place when you see Abraham and Isaac and Jacob and all the prophets in the kingdom of God – but not you. Other people will come from east and west and north and south and recline at the table in the kingdom of God. Surprisingly, some who think they will be last will be first, and some who think they will be first will actually be last."

[101]Just then, some Pharisees came and said to him, "You better get out of here. You know Herod wants to kill you."

---

[100]Luke 13:22-30
[101]Matthew 23:37-39; Luke 13:31-35

"You go and tell that fox, 'I cast out demons and heal people today and tomorrow, and I will finish up on the third day.' Still, I must keep going today and tomorrow and the next day because we can't have a prophet dying outside of Jerusalem."

"O Jerusalem, Jerusalem, the city that kills the prophets and stones those who are sent to it! How many times I wanted to gather your children together as a hen gathers her chicks under her wings, but you wouldn't do it. Look, now your house is left to you as a forsaken desert because I'm telling you, you won't see me again until you say, [102]*Blessed is he who comes in the name of the Lord.*"

[103]One Sabbath day, he went to have dinner at the house of a ruler of the Pharisees, and they were watching him carefully. A man came and stood in front of him. He had a condition that caused him to be very swollen from body fluids. So Jesus responded to the lawyers and Pharisees by saying, "Does the Law let us heal on the Sabbath or not?"

They didn't say a word. Jesus healed the man and sent him on his way and said to them, "If your son or your ox falls into a well on a Sabbath day, will you pull him out? Which one of you won't?" They would not answer the question.

Jesus noticed how those who were invited to dinner chose to sit in the places of honor, so he told a story. He said, "When you're invited to a wedding feast, don't sit down in a place of honor, for someone more distinguished than you who has been invited may come in, and the one who invited you both will come and say to you, 'I need you to get up and give your place to this person,' and then you will be ashamed to go sit in the common seats. Instead, when you are invited, go first and sit in the lowest place, so that when your host comes he might say to you, 'My friend, come move to a better seat.' Then everyone sitting at the table will see you

---

[102] Psalm 118:26
[103] Luke 14:1-35

honored. Because everyone who honors himself will be humbled, and everyone who humbles himself will be honored."

Then Jesus spoke to the man who had invited him and said, "The next time you give a lunch or a dinner, don't invite your friends, brothers, relatives, or rich neighbors. They'll just invite you back and you'll be repaid in kind. For your next dinner, invite the poor, the crippled, the lame, and the blind. You will be blessed because they can't repay you, but you will be repaid when the just are resurrected."

Hearing Jesus talk like this made one of those sitting at the table exclaim, "Blessed is everyone who will eat bread in the kingdom of God!"

But Jesus replied, "A man once held a great banquet and invited a lot of people. At dinner time, he sent his servant to tell those who had been invited, 'You can come over now, everything is ready.'

The first guest said, 'Please excuse me, I have to go and see a field I bought.' Another person said, 'I have to go and check on the five yoke of oxen I just bought, please pardon me.' Another gave the excuse, 'I just got married and I can't come.' When the servant came back and reported these things to his master, the master became angry. He told him, 'I want you to go to the streets and the alleys of the city and bring back the poor and crippled and blind and lame – and hurry!' The servant replied, 'Sir, we've already done that, and there's still plenty of room left.' And the master said, 'Then go out to the highways and to the boundary walls, to the homeless, and convince people to come in so that my house will be filled. But, I'll guarantee this – none of the people who were originally invited will even taste my food.'"

Along the way, great crowds were with him, and he turned to them and said, "If anyone comes to me and does not hate his own father and mother and wife and children and brothers and sisters, and yes, even his own life, he cannot be my disciple. Whoever does not carry his own cross and come after me cannot be my disciple."

"Consider this: which one of you, if you wanted to build a tower, would not sit down first and figure up the cost, so you would know if you have enough to finish it? If you don't, and you can't finish after laying the foundation, people who see it will make fun of you, saying, 'He started building, but he couldn't even finish it.' Or what king, who is going to war with another king, does not sit down first and determine if he is able to fight twenty thousand men with only his ten thousand? Then if he decides he can't, he sends a delegation while the other is still far away to make a peace treaty. In a similar way, you cannot be my disciple unless you renounce all that you have."

"You see, salt is good, but if it loses its taste, how are you going to make it salty again? It's worthless, and you can't use it for the soil or manure pile – you just throw it away. He who has ears to hear, let him hear."

[104]The tax collectors and sinners all gathered in close to hear him. This caused the Pharisees and the scribes to grumble, "This man accepts sinners and even eats with them."

Then Jesus was moved to tell this story: "If you had a hundred sheep, and you lost one of them, which one of you wouldn't leave the ninety-nine in the open field and go search for the lost one until you found it? And the one who found it would carry it home on his shoulders rejoicing, and when he got home he would call his friends and neighbors and say, 'Be happy with me since I found my lost sheep.' It's just like that in Heaven – they are happier over one sinner who repents than over ninety-nine righteous people who don't need to."

"Or what about a woman who loses one of her ten silver coins? Don't you think she will light a lamp and sweep the house and turn it upside down until she finds it? And when she finds it, she calls her friends and neighbors to come over, saying, 'Rejoice with me because I found my lost money.' I'm

---

[104]Luke 15:1-32

telling you, it's the same way when the angels of God see the happiness that follows when one sinner repents."

To further make his point, he told this story: "There was a man who had two sons. The younger son said to his father, 'Dad, I want you to give me my inheritance now.' So his dad divided the property between them.

"Not long after this, the younger son packed up all he had and went far away to another country where he squandered his inheritance through reckless living. When he had wasted it all, a severe famine hit the land, so he took a job with one of the citizens in that country who hired him to feed his pigs. He was so poor that he wished he could eat the pigs' food. No one else would give him anything."

"One day he came to himself and said, 'How many of my father's employees have more than enough bread, while I am starving to death! I'm going to get up and go home to my daddy, and I am going to tell him, "Dad, I know I sinned against Heaven and you. I'm no longer worthy to be called your son. Just let me be one of your hired hands." He got up and headed home to his dad. While he was still a long way off, his father saw him and with a gut-wrenching compassion began running to him. His dad hugged him and kissed him as his son said, 'Dad, I know I've sinned against Heaven and you, and I'm not worthy to be called your son.' But his father turned to his workers and said, 'I want you to hurry. Bring me the best robe I've got and put it on him. I also want you to get shoes, and put a ring on his finger. Then go get the fattened calf ready to eat. Today we celebrate because my son was dead, and now he's alive again! He was lost, but now he is found!' And they began to celebrate."

"Now his older son was in the field, and as he was coming home, he could hear music and dancing. He called one of the servants and asked what was going on. He replied, 'Your brother has come home, and your dad killed the fattened calf because he got his son back safe and sound.' This made the older son angry and he refused to go in. His dad came out and asked him what was going on. 'Look!' he answered. 'All these years I have served you, and I never disobeyed you, but you never gave me a goat so I could have a party with my friends. But when this son of yours returned, who has thrown away your property on prostitutes, you went all out for him!' And his dad said to him, 'Son, you are always with me, and I share everything I have with you. But it was fitting to celebrate and be glad because your brother was dead and now he's alive! He was lost, and now he is found!'"

[105]He also told the disciples this story: "There was a rich man who had a manager, and someone came and accused the manager of wasting the rich man's possessions. He called the manager in and asked him, 'What's this I'm hearing about you? Turn in your account books – you're fired.' And the manager said to himself, 'What am I going to do since my boss is firing me? I'm not strong enough for manual labor, and I'm too proud to beg. I know what I'll do so that when I'm jobless, people will still accept me into their homes.' He called his boss' debtors one by one and he asked the first, 'How much do you owe my boss?' He answered, 'Eight hundred gallons of oil.' He said to him, 'Quick, take your bill, sit down and write another invoice for four hundred gallons instead.' Then he asked another, 'How much do you owe?' He replied, 'A thousand bushels of wheat.' He said to him, 'Take your bill and write it for eight hundred bushels instead.' The employer had to applaud the crooked manager for his shrewdness. You see, the children of this world are more clever in dealing with their own generation than the children of light. I tell you, use worldly wealth to make friends for yourselves, so that when it runs out, they may receive you into the homes of the coming age."

"A person who is faithful in a little thing will be faithful in a big thing, and a person who is dishonest in a little thing will be dishonest in a big thing. If you have not been faithful with worldly wealth, who is going to trust you with true

---

[105]Luke 16:1-17, 19-31

riches? And if you have not been faithful with other people's things, who will give you your own stuff? No servant can serve two masters. He's going to hate one and love the other or be devoted to one and despise the other. You cannot serve God and money."

The Pharisees heard all these things, and because they loved money, they ridiculed Jesus. He responded harshly, saying, "You know how to make yourselves look good before men, but God knows your hearts. What men value the most is an abomination in God's sight."

"Up until the time of John we had the Law and the Prophets, but since then the good news of the kingdom of God has been preached, and everyone must force their way into it. Still, it is easier for Heaven and Earth to pass away than for one dot of the Law to fail."

"There was a rich man who dressed in the best clothes and ate like a king every day. Outside his gate, a poor man named Lazarus was laid there, covered in sores, wishing he could eat what fell off the rich man's table. Only the dogs came, and they licked his sores. One day the poor man died and the angels came and carried him to be with Abraham. The rich man died too, and he was buried and went to Hell. There, he looked up in torment and saw Abraham far away with Lazarus by his side.

He yelled out, 'Father Abraham, have mercy on me, and send Lazarus to dip his finger in water and cool my tongue. The pain of this fire is too much.' Abraham replied, 'Child, don't you remember that you received good things in your lifetime? And don't you remember how Lazarus, on the other hand, had it so bad? Yet, now he is comforted here, and you are tormented there. Besides all this, look at this massive gulf between us. It was put here so no one could get to the other side.' Still the rich man pleaded, 'Then father, I'm begging you, please send Lazarus to my dad's house. I've got five brothers there. Please let him go warn them so they won't wind up in this torment.' But Abraham said, 'They already have Moses and the Prophets; they can listen to them.' And he said, 'No, father Abraham, but if someone goes to them from the dead, then they will change their ways.' But Abraham declared, 'If they won't listen to Moses and the Prophets, they won't be convinced even if someone rises from the dead.'"

[106]Jesus taught his disciples more when he said, "You will certainly be tempted to sin, but it will be very bad for the person who actually brings the temptations to people. In fact, it would be better for him if a millstone were hung around his neck and he were thrown into the sea than for him to cause one of these little ones to sin. Pay attention to yourselves!"

"If your brother sins, confront him. If he's truly sorry, forgive him, and if he sins against you seven times in a day and comes back to you seven times, saying, 'I'm truly sorry,' then you should forgive him."

The apostles said to the Lord, "Make our faith bigger!"

"If you had faith like a grain of mustard seed," said Jesus, "you could tell this mulberry tree, 'Go jump in that lake,' and it would obey you."

"Is there a single one of you who has a servant plowing or tending sheep, who would say to him when he comes in from the field, 'First, come relax at the table'? Instead, won't you say to him, 'Get dressed, cook supper, and serve it to me, and after that you can have your meal'? And, do you thank the servant because he did what he was told to do? So when you have done all you were commanded to do, you should also say, 'We're just typical servants, and we only did what we were supposed to.'"

+ + +

[107]A man named Lazarus was sick. He lived in the village of Bethany along with his sisters, Mary and Martha. Mary was

---

[106]Luke 17:1-10
[107]John 11:1-57

the one who anointed the Lord with ointment and wiped his feet with her hair. The sisters sent for Jesus, saying, "Lord, the one you love is sick."

When Jesus heard it, he said, "This illness does not lead to death. It is for the glory of God, so the Son of God may be glorified through it."

Jesus loved Martha and her sister and Lazarus. Yet, when he heard that Lazarus was ill, he stayed where he was for two more days. After this, he said to the disciples, "Let's go back to Judea."

The disciples asked, "Rabbi, do you really want to go back there since the Jews just tried to stone you?"

"Aren't there still twelve hours in a day?" Jesus asked them. "If anyone walks in the day, he doesn't stumble because he sees the light of this world. But if anyone walks in the night, he stumbles because the light is not in him."

After saying these things, he said, "Our friend Lazarus has fallen asleep, but I'm going to wake him up."

"Lord, if he has fallen asleep, he'll recover," the disciples reasoned.

Jesus was talking about death, but they thought that he meant resting in sleep. Then Jesus made it plain, "Lazarus has died, and I am glad for your sake that I wasn't there. This way it will help you believe. Now it's time to go to him."

And Thomas, the one called the Twin, said to his fellow disciples, "Let's go with him, that way we can all die together."

When Jesus arrived, he discovered that Lazarus had already been in the tomb for four days. Bethany was near Jerusalem, about two miles away, and many of the Jews had come to console Martha and Mary over their brother.

When Martha heard that Jesus was coming, she met him on the way, but Mary sat in the house. Martha said to Jesus, "Lord, if you had been here, my brother would not have died, but even now I know that God will give you whatever you ask."

"Your brother will rise again," Jesus replied.

"I know that," said Martha. "He will rise again in the resurrection on the last day."

"I am the resurrection and the life," said Jesus. "Whoever believes in me will live, even when he dies, and everyone who lives and believes in me will never die. Do you believe this?"

"Yes Lord, I believe that you are the Messiah, the Son of God, who is coming into the world."

After she had said this, she went and called her sister Mary and told her privately, "The Teacher is here and he's calling for you."

She got up quickly and went to Jesus who had not yet come into the village, but was still in the place where Martha had met him. The Jews who were comforting her in the house saw Mary leave hurriedly, so they followed her, assuming that she was going to weep at the tomb. When she got to Jesus and saw him, she fell at his feet saying, "Lord, if you had been here, my brother would not have died."

When Jesus saw Mary crying and the Jews who had come with her crying too, it moved him deep down in his spirit and troubled him. "Where have you laid him?" he asked.

"Lord, come and see."

Jesus began to cry.

"See how much he loved him!" said the Jews.

But some said, "If he could open the eyes of the blind man, why couldn't he keep this man from dying?"

Jesus was disturbed as he arrived at the tomb. It was a cave, and a stone was over it. "Move the stone out of the way," Jesus said.

"Lord," said Martha, "he's been dead for four days; it will stink now."

"Didn't I tell you that if you believed you would see the glory of God?"

They moved the stone and Jesus looked up and said, "Father, thank you for hearing me. I know that you always do, but I want these people standing here to benefit from hearing it and believe that you sent me."

After saying this, he shouted, "Lazarus, come out!"

The man who had died came out with his hands and feet wrapped in linen strips and his face wrapped in a cloth. "Unwrap him and let him go," said Jesus.

As a result, many of the Jews who had come with Mary and had seen what he did, believed in him. But some of them went to the Pharisees and told them what Jesus had done. Then the chief priests and the Pharisees gathered the Council and said, "We have to do something – this man keeps performing miracles, and if that continues, everyone will believe in him, and the Romans will come and take away our place and our nation."

Then Caiaphas, who was high priest that year, said to them, "You are all so dense. You don't realize that it's better if one man dies for the people, rather than the whole nation die."

He didn't just come up with this on his own, but being high priest that year, he was saying – before it happened – that Jesus would die for the nation, and that his death would bring together all of God's children who were scattered abroad. From that day on, they made plans to kill him.

Therefore, Jesus no longer walked publicly among the Jews. He left for the region near the desert to stay with the disciples in a town called Ephraim.

It was almost time for the Jewish Passover, and many people went up from the country to Jerusalem beforehand to purify themselves. They were looking for Jesus and talking as they stood around in the temple, saying, "What do you think? Do you think he won't come to the feast at all?" The chief priests and the Pharisees had given orders that if anyone knew where he was, they should report it to them, so they could arrest him.

[108]Later, the Pharisees wanted to know when the kingdom of God would come. Jesus answered them, "The kingdom of God is not coming with signs you can see, and you won't be able to say, 'Look, here it is!' or 'There it is!' Instead, look around! The kingdom of God is all around you." And he said to the disciples, "The day will come when you will long to see one of the days of the Son of Man, but you won't see it. They will say to you, 'Look, there it is!' or 'Look, it's here!' Don't go, and don't follow them. Just like lightning flashes and lights up the sky from one side to the other, that's how the Son of Man will be in his day. But first he must suffer many things and be rejected by this generation. The days of the Son of Man will be just like the days of Noah. They were eating and drinking and marrying, right up until the day Noah entered the ark, and the flood came and destroyed them all. It was similar to that in Lot's time when they were eating, drinking, buying, selling, planting, and building. Then on the day when Lot left Sodom, fire and sulfur rained from Heaven and destroyed them all, and that's just how it will be on the day when the Son of Man is revealed. On that day, the one who is on the housetop better not come down to try to rescue his things out of his house. Also, the one in the field should not turn back. Remember what happened to Lot's wife. So whoever tries to save his life will lose it, but whoever loses his life will keep it. I'm telling you, in that night, two people will be in one bed. One will be taken and the other will be left. There will be two women grinding grain together. One will be taken and the other will be left."

They asked him, "Where, Lord?"

"The vultures will gather where the dead bodies are," he answered.

---

[108]Luke 17:20-37

[109]And he told them a story to illustrate the point that they should pray all the time and never lose heart. He said, "There was a city where the judge didn't fear God or respect people. And there was a widow in that city who kept coming to him and saying, 'Give me justice against my enemy.' For a while he ignored her, but afterward he said to himself, 'I'm not afraid of God and I don't care about anybody, but this widow is driving me crazy! I'm going to give her justice so she will get off my back and stop coming here every day.'" And the Lord said, "Listen to what this worldly judge is saying. Now, won't God give justice to his chosen ones who cry to him every night and day? Will he just put them off? No, I'm telling you, he will give them swift justice. On the other hand, when the Son of Man comes, will he find faith on Earth?"

Jesus told another parable to some who had assured themselves of their own righteousness as they looked down on other people:

"Two men went up into the temple to pray. One man was a Pharisee and the other was a tax collector. The Pharisee stood by himself and prayed, 'God, I thank you that I am not like other men – swindlers, unjust, adulterers, or even like this tax collector. I fast twice a week, and I tithe on all my income.' But the tax collector stood far off and wouldn't even look up to Heaven. Instead, he beat on his chest, repeating, 'God have mercy on me, I am such a sinner!' I tell you, this man went home righteous, not the other one. Every person who honors himself will be humbled, but the one who humbles himself will be honored."

[110]Later, the Pharisees came and tested him by asking, "Does the Law allow a man to divorce his wife for any reason he chooses?"

"What did Moses command you?" he answered.

---

[109]Luke 18:1-14
[110]Mark 10:2-12; Matthew 19:3-12; Luke 16:18

117

"Moses allowed a man to write a certificate of divorce and send her away," they said.

Jesus replied, "But their creator made them male and female from the beginning, and said: [111]*This is why a man will leave his father and his mother and not let go of his wife, and they shall become one flesh.* Have you not read that? They are no longer two – but one flesh. Whatever God has joined together, man should not separate."

"Then why did Moses command husbands to give wives a certificate of divorce and send them away?" they asked.

"He wrote you this commandment because of your hard hearts. He allowed you to divorce your wives, but that's not how it was from the beginning."

Once they were in the house, the disciples wanted to know more about divorce. So Jesus said, "Whoever divorces his wife, except for sexual immorality, and marries someone else commits adultery against her. And if she divorces her husband and marries someone else, they commit adultery."

The disciples said to him, "If that's the way it is between a man and his wife, then it's better not to marry."

Jesus replied this way, "Not everyone can accept your conclusion of not marrying. Only those who are given the ability can do that. There are people who don't marry because they were born with no desire, others were castrated, and there are some who choose not to for the sake of the kingdom of Heaven. This is only for those who say, 'Being single works for me.'"

[112]People were bringing children, even infants, to him because they wanted him to lay his hands on them and pray. When the disciples saw it, they tried to stop the people. This bothered Jesus, and he said, "Do not stop these children from coming to me; the kingdom of God belongs to them. If you want to know the truth – whoever does not receive the

---

[111] Genesis 2:24
[112] Mark 10:13-31; Matthew 19:13-30; Luke 18:15-30

kingdom of God like a child will not enter it!" He called them back to him and laid his hands on some and held others in his arms and blessed them. After this, he left.

As he was leaving for a trip, a ruler ran up and knelt down in front of him and asked, "Good Teacher, what good deed must I do to inherit the life of the ages?"

"Why are you calling me good? God is the only one who is good," Jesus replied. "If you want that kind of life, keep the commandments."

"Which ones?" he asked.

"'Don't murder, don't commit adultery, don't steal, don't lie, don't cheat, honor your father and mother, and love your neighbor like you love yourself.'"

"Teacher, I've done all of these things since I was young. Am I missing anything?" the young man said.

Jesus was looking at him – he loved him – so he told him this: "You are missing one thing. If you want to be perfect, go sell everything you own, take the money and give it all to the poor, and you will have treasure in Heaven. Then, come follow me."

When the young man heard this, his heart sank – it made him terribly sad, and he walked away because he was extremely rich.

Jesus saw that he had become sad; he looked around and said to his disciples, "It is very hard for rich people to enter God's kingdom!"

The disciples were stunned by his words. Jesus repeated it: "Children, it is hard to get into the kingdom of God! A camel can go through the eye of a needle easier than a rich person can get into the kingdom of God.

This astonished them, and they wondered out loud, "Then who can be saved?"

Jesus looked at them and said, "Well, it's impossible with man, but not with God. God can do anything."

Then Peter spoke up, "Look at us, we have left our homes and everything to follow you. So what do we get?"

Jesus said, "The truth is – in the new world, when the Son of Man sits on his glorious throne, you men who have followed me will also sit on twelve thrones judging the twelve tribes of Israel. And everyone who has left house or brothers or sisters or mother or father or children or land for my name's sake, for the kingdom of God, and for the gospel, will receive a hundred times as much now in this time. They'll receive houses and brothers and sisters and mothers and children and lands, along with persecutions. Finally, in the time to come, they'll get the life of the ages. However, many who are first will be last, and the last will be first."

[113]They continued toward Jerusalem as Jesus walked up ahead of the amazed disciples and others who were following but afraid. Then Jesus paused to take the twelve aside and he began to tell them what was going to happen to him: "See, we are going up to Jerusalem, and everything that is written about the Son of Man by the prophets is going to happen. He will be handed over to the chief priests and the scribes, and they will condemn him to death and deliver him over to the Gentiles. Then they will mock him and spit on him and abuse him horribly. After they flog him, they will kill him by crucifixion, and on the third day, he will rise from the dead."

None of this made any sense to them. What Jesus was telling them was hidden from them, and they did not understand him.

Then the mother of Zebedee's sons came up to him with her sons, James and John. She knelt down before him to ask him for something as James and John said, "Teacher, we want you to do whatever we ask you to do for us."

"What do you want?" Jesus said to their mom.

"Tell me that these two sons of mine will sit at your right and left hand in your kingdom."

"What do you want me to do for you?" he also asked her sons.

---

[113]Mark 10:32-45; Matthew 20:17-28; Luke 18:31-34

"Tell us that we can sit on your right and left hand in your glory."

"You have no idea what you're asking for. Are you able to drink the cup I drink, or to be immersed with the baptism I'm immersed with?"

"Yes, we are," they replied.

"You will drink the cup that I drink, and you will be immersed with the same baptism as myself, but who sits at my right or left is not my decision. Those places are decided by my Father."

The other ten heard this and were angry with James and John. So Jesus called them all together and said, "You know that Gentile rulers use their positions against the people, and their leaders exercise authority over them. But it can't be that way with you. Instead, whoever wants to be great will do it by being everyone's servant, and whoever wants to be first among you must be everyone's slave. It's the same with the Son of Man – he didn't come to be served, but to serve, and to give his life as a ransom for many."

[114]One day, he was approaching Jericho and a blind man was sitting by the roadside, begging. He heard the crowd passing and asked someone what was going on.

"Jesus of Nazareth is coming through here," they told him. Jesus continued on through Jericho and a rich man named Zacchaeus, a chief tax collector, was there. He was trying to see Jesus, but he was too short to see over the crowd. He ran up ahead and climbed into a sycamore tree to see Jesus, just as he was about to pass by. As Jesus came close, he looked up and said, "Zacchaeus, hurry and come down so I can stay at your house today."

He climbed down in a hurry, excited to take Jesus to his home. Those who saw it were grumbling, "That man is a sinner, and Jesus went to be his guest."

---

[114]Luke 19:1-27

121

Zacchaeus stood up and said to the Lord, "Lord, I am giving half of all I have to the poor. On top of that, I will restore to anyone I cheated, four times as much as I took."

"Today," Jesus said, "salvation has come to this house, to a son of Abraham because the Son of Man came to seek and to save the lost."

Since he was close to Jerusalem and the people thought the kingdom of God was suddenly about to appear, Jesus decided to tell a parable. He said, "A man of high standing went into a far country to receive a kingdom and then return home. He called ten of his servants and gave each of them ten minas, or about six months' salary, and said to them, 'Take care of business until I get back.' The problem was that his citizens hated him and sent a delegation after him to say, 'We do not want this man to reign over us.' When he returned after receiving the kingdom, he had the servants called in to hear how much they had made while he was gone. The first came in to say, 'Lord, your money has made ten times as much.' 'Great job,' he said, 'Now that's a good servant! Because you have been faithful in something small you will be given authority over ten cities.' Then the second came in and said, 'Lord, your money has made five times as much.' So he said to him, 'You are to be over five cities.' Then another came in saying, 'Lord, here is your money. I have kept it put up in a handkerchief because I was afraid of you since you are a hard man to deal with. You take what you do not deposit and reap what you do not sow.' The man replied, 'You wicked servant; your own words condemn you! You knew how hard a man I am, taking what I do not deposit and reaping what I do not sow. Why didn't you put my money in the bank so I could have made the interest?' And the owner said to the bystanders, 'Take the money from him and give it to the one who has the ten minas.' And they reminded him, 'Lord, he already has ten minas!' 'Yes, and more will be given to everyone who already has some, but from the one who doesn't have, even what he does have will be taken away. But as for my enemies who didn't want me to reign over them, bring them here and slaughter them in front of me.'"

[115]Later, as Jesus left Jericho with his disciples and a great crowd, there were two blind men sitting by the roadside begging. One was Bartimaeus, the son of Timaeus. One of them asked what was going on. "Jesus of Nazareth is passing by," he was told.

They started crying out, "Lord Jesus!"

"Son of David!"

"Have mercy on us!"

The people who were in front rebuked them, telling them to be quiet, but they just shouted louder, "Son of David!"

"Lord!"

"Have mercy on us!"

Jesus stopped and said, "Tell them to come here."

So they called to them, "Get up and be encouraged; he is calling you." Bartimaeus jumped up, threw his coat down and came to Jesus.

"What do you want me to do for you?" Jesus asked.

"Rabbi, let me have my sight back," he answered, as both men said, "Lord, make our eyes see again."

"Let your sight come back to you now," Jesus said with pity as he touched their eyes. "Now you can go where you want to. Your faith has made you well." Immediately, they could see. And they followed him, glorifying God as did all the people who saw this.

[116]Six days before the Passover, Jesus came to Bethany where he had raised Lazarus from the dead. Dinner had been prepared for him at Simon the leper's house. Martha served, and Lazarus was one of those reclining at the table with him. At some point, Mary came up to him with a very expensive alabaster flask of perfume, a pound of pure nard, and she

---

[115]Mark 10:46-52; Matthew 20:29-34; Luke 18:35-43
[116]Mark 14:3-9; Matthew 26:6-13; John 12:1-11

broke the flask and poured it over his head. Then she anointed the feet of Jesus and wiped them with her hair. The fragrance filled the house along with the indignation of some who said to themselves, "Why would you waste perfume like that? Especially when it could have been sold for a lot of money and given to the poor."

And they scolded her.

Then Judas Iscariot, the disciple who was about to betray him, said, "Why was this perfume not sold for three hundred days salary and given to the poor?"

He said this not because he cared about the poor, but because he was a thief, and as the one who managed the disciples' common purse, he would help himself to what was in it.

Jesus said, "Why are you giving her a hard time? Leave her alone. She has done a beautiful thing for me, and anytime you want to do good for the poor, they will always be waiting for you. However, you won't always have me. She has kept this for the day of my burial, and now by pouring this perfume, she has done what she could to anoint my body and prepare me for burial. And the truth is – wherever the gospel is told anywhere in the whole world, they will tell what she has done in memory of her."

Meanwhile, many of the Jews found out that Jesus was there and a big crowd came, not only for him, but also to see Lazarus since he had been raised from the dead. So the chief priests were planning to kill Lazarus as well because he was the reason many of the Jews were going away and believing in Jesus.

The Last Days: Jerusalem

[117]The next day as they came nearer to Jerusalem, they arrived at the Mount of Olives in Bethpage and Bethany. Jesus sent two of his disciples, saying, "Go into the village before you, and just as you get there you'll find a donkey tied up, and a colt with her, which no one has ever ridden. Untie them and bring them to me. If anyone asks, 'What are you doing?' say, 'The Lord needs these and will return them very soon.'" This happened in order to fulfill what the prophet said,

> [118]*Say to the daughter of Zion,*
> *'Behold, your king is coming to you,*
> *humble and mounted on a donkey,*
> *and on a colt, the foal of a beast of burden.*

They went and found a colt tied at a door outside in the street, like he said, and while they were untying it, its owners asked, "Why are you untying the colt?"

"The Lord needs it," they responded as Jesus had directed them. So they let them go, and they brought the donkey and the colt to Jesus. Then they laid their coats on the colt and sat Jesus on it.

On the way down the Mount of Olives, and the closer they got to Jerusalem, the whole crowd of his followers began to rejoice loudly and to praise God for all the mighty works they had seen, saying,

"Blessed is the King who comes in the name of the Lord!"

"Peace in Heaven and glory in the highest!"

But some of the Pharisees in the crowd said, "Teacher, rebuke your disciples!"

---

[117]Mark 11:1-11; Matthew 21:1-11; Luke 19:28-44; John 12:12-19
[118] Zechariah 9:9

"I tell you," he said, "if they get quiet, the rocks will start shouting!"

Along with this, the big crowd that had come to the feast also heard that Jesus was coming to Jerusalem. Many of them started spreading their coats on the road, and others spread palm tree and other leafy branches they cut from the fields. The crowds ahead of and behind him were shouting,

"Hosanna to the Son of David!"

[119]*"Blessed is he who comes in the name of the Lord!"*

"Don't be afraid daughter of Zion. Look! Your king is coming, sitting on a donkey's colt!"

"Blessed is the coming kingdom of our father David – and the King of Israel!"

"Hosanna in the highest!"

But Jesus started crying as he came closer to the city. "Oh how I wish that you, especially you, knew the things that would bring you peace today! Yet now they are hidden from your eyes, and the days will come when your enemies will surround you with blockades and hem you in on every side and tear you down to the ground – you and your children. They won't leave one stone on another because you didn't recognize the time of your visitation."

He continued on into Jerusalem and the whole city was stirred up saying, "Who is this?"

"This is the prophet Jesus from Nazareth of Galilee," the crowds answered.

Then he went into the temple. He looked around at everything, and since it was already late, he left for Bethany with the twelve.

His disciples did not understand all this at first, but after Jesus was glorified, they remembered that these things had been written about him and done to him.

Meanwhile, the crowd that had been with him when he called Lazarus out of the tomb and raised him from the dead

---

[119] Psalm 118:26; Zechariah 9:9

126

continued to witness to it all. That's the reason they all went out to meet him. So the Pharisees complained to one another, "You see, you're not accomplishing anything. Look, the world has gone after him!"

[120]There were also some Greeks who went up to worship at the feast, and they came to Philip, who was from Bethsaida in Galilee, and said, "Sir, we want to see Jesus."

Philip went and told Andrew, and they went and told Jesus. He answered, "It is time for the Son of Man to be glorified, and the truth is – unless a grain of wheat falls into the earth and dies, it remains one seed. But if it dies, it bears much fruit. Whoever loves his life will lose it, and whoever hates his life in this world will keep it. He will have the life of the ages. If you want to serve me, you have to follow me; then my servant will be wherever I am, and my Father will honor anyone who serves me."

"Now I have a troubled soul and what can I say? 'Dad, save me from this hour?' But this hour is why I came here, so Father, glorify your name."

"I have glorified it, and I will glorify it again," came a voice from Heaven.

The crowd standing there heard it and thought it had thundered, while others said, "An angel spoke to him."

Jesus said, "This voice was for you, not me. This world will be judged now, and now the ruler of this world will be thrown out. And I – when I am lifted up from the earth – will draw all people to myself." He said this to show the kind of death he was going to die.

Then the crowd answered him, "But the Messiah will live forever, at least that's what we understood the Law to say. So how can you say that the Son of Man must be lifted up? Who is this Son of Man?"

"The light is among you for a little while longer," Jesus replied. "Walk while you have the light or darkness will

---

[120]John 12:20-50

overtake you. The one who walks in the darkness does not know where he is going. While you have the light, believe in the light. That's how you become sons of light."

After saying all this, Jesus left and hid from them. No matter how many miracles he had done, they still didn't believe in him. This fulfilled what the prophet Isaiah said: [121]*Lord, who has believed what we said, and to whom has the arm of the Lord been revealed?* That's why they couldn't believe, as Isaiah also said, *He has blinded their eyes and hardened their heart, so they won't see with their eyes and understand with their heart and turn, and I would heal them.*

Isaiah spoke these things because he saw his glory and talked about him. Nevertheless, there were quite a number of authorities who believed in him, yet they kept it quiet because they were too afraid of the Pharisees and didn't want to be kicked out of the synagogue. They loved the glory that comes from man more than the glory that comes from God.

Then Jesus cried out, "Whoever believes in me isn't believing in me, but in him who sent me. And whoever sees me is seeing the one who sent me. I have come into the world as light, so that whoever believes in me won't stay in the dark. If anyone hears what I say and does not obey it, I don't judge him. I did not come to judge the world, but to save it. The one who rejects me and does not receive what I say has a judge. The word that I have spoken will judge him on the last day because I have not spoken on my own authority, but the Father who sent me gave me a commandment – what to say and what to speak. I know that his commandment is the life of the ages. So I say what the Father told me to say."

[122] During the morning on the next day when they came from Bethany, Jesus was hungry. Along the way, he saw a fig tree in the distance. It was in leaf, and he went to see if he

---

[121] Isaiah 53:1; 6:10
[122] Mark 11:12-26; Matthew 21:12-22; Luke 19:45-48

could find anything on it, but he only found leaves because it wasn't the season for figs.

"May no one ever eat fruit from you again," his disciples heard him say, and they traveled on to Jerusalem. He entered the temple there and began to drive out the temple buyers and sellers, and he turned over the moneychangers' tables and the seats of those who sold pigeons. He wouldn't even allow anyone to carry anything through the temple, and he was teaching and saying, "Is it not written: [123]*My house shall be called a house of prayer for all people?* But you have turned it into a robbers' den."

This kind of talk made the chief priests, scribes, and leaders of the people search for a way to destroy him. They were afraid of him because the entire crowd was amazed by his teaching. Still, there was nothing they could do since the people were hanging on his every word.

He was teaching daily, and the blind and the lame came to him in the temple and he healed them. But when the chief priests and the scribes saw the amazing things that he did and heard the kids yelling in the temple, "Hosanna to the Son of David!" they were offended.

"Do you hear what they are saying?"

"Yes." said Jesus, "Haven't you read, [124]*You bring praise out of the mouths of infants and nursing babies?*"

That evening he left them, set out from the city, and went to stay in Bethany. As they returned in the morning, they saw the fig tree withered to its roots. Peter remembered and said, "Rabbi, look! The fig tree that you cursed has withered."

When the disciples saw it they marveled, asking, "How did the fig tree wither all at once?"

"Have faith in God," answered Jesus, "and you will not only do what has been done to the fig tree, but the truth is –

---

[123] Isaiah 56:7; Jeremiah 7:11
[124] Psalm 8:2

whoever says to this mountain, 'Go throw yourself in the sea,' and does not doubt in his heart but believes that what he says will happen – it will be done for him. So I'm telling you, whatever you ask in prayer, believe that you have received it, and it will be yours. And whenever you stand praying, if you have anything against anyone, forgive them so that your Father who is in Heaven may forgive you your trespasses."

[125]Once again, they returned to Jerusalem, and as he was walking in the temple and teaching and preaching the gospel, the chief priests, scribes, and elders came and they said to him, "By what authority are you doing these things, or who gave you this power to do them?"

"I'll ask you one question," Jesus replied, "and if you tell me the answer, I will tell you by what authority I do these things. Was the baptism of John from Heaven or from man? Answer me."

They talked it over, saying, "If we say, 'From Heaven,' he will say, 'Then why didn't you believe him?' But if we say, 'From man,' we're afraid the people will stone us to death because they all believe John was a prophet."

So they answered Jesus, "We don't know."

"Then I won't tell you by what authority I do these things."

[126]And he started speaking to them in parables. "What do you think? A man had two sons, and he went to the first and said, 'Son, go work in the vineyard today.' He answered, 'I won't do it,' but a little later he changed his mind and went. The father asked the same of his other son, who answered, 'Yes sir, I'm on my way,' but he did not go. Which of the two did the father's will?"

"The first," they said.

"The truth is – " Jesus began, "the tax collectors and the prostitutes get into the kingdom of God before you. That's

---

[125]Mark 11:27-33; Matthew 21:23-27; Luke 20:1-8
[126]Mark 12:1-12; Matthew 21:28-46; Luke 20:9-18

because John came to you in the way of righteousness, and you did not believe him, but the tax collectors and the prostitutes believed him. And even when you saw it, you didn't change your minds 'a little later' and believe him."

"Listen to another parable: There was a master of a house who planted a vineyard, put a fence around it, dug a pit for the winepress, and built a tower. He leased it to tenants and went into another country. When the season came, he sent his servants to the tenants to get some of the fruit of the vineyard from them. But the tenants took his servants and beat one of them and sent him away empty-handed. They also killed one and stoned another. So he sent more servants than he did the first time, and they did the same to them. Then he sent another and they killed him. This went on with many others; they beat some and killed others. Yet, the master had one other – a son he loved very much. Finally, he sent him to them, saying, 'They will respect my son.' Instead, those tenants said, 'This is the heir. Come on, if we kill him, the inheritance will be ours.' So they killed him and threw him out of the vineyard. What do you think the owner of the vineyard will do to those tenants when he comes?"

"He will put those evil men to a horrible death and lease the vineyard to other tenants who will give him the fruits on time," some said. And Jesus agreed.

Others said, "No way!"

But he looked directly at them and said, "Then why is it written, [127]*The stone that the builders rejected has become the cornerstone; the Lord did this, and it is marvelous in our eyes*"?

"I'm telling you, the kingdom of God will be taken away from you and given to people producing its fruits. Anyone who falls on this stone will be broken in pieces, and when it falls on anyone it will grind him to dust."

When the chief priests and the Pharisees heard his stories, they knew he was talking about them. They tried to

---

[127] Psalm 118:22

find a way to arrest him right then, but they were too afraid of the crowds who thought he was a prophet, so they left.

[128]Jesus continued, telling the people another story. He said, "You can compare the kingdom of Heaven to a king who threw a wedding party for his son. He sent his servants to call those who were invited, but they wouldn't come. Again, he sent other servants saying, 'Tell those who are invited, 'Look, the dinner is ready, my oxen and cattle have been slaughtered, and everything is ready, come on, let's celebrate.' But no one paid any attention. They just left, one to his farm and another to his business, while the rest kidnapped his servants, treated them horribly, and killed them. The king was furious. He sent his troops and destroyed those murderers and burned their city. Then he said to his servants, 'The wedding party is still ready, but those invited were not worthy. This time, go out to the main highway and invite to the party as many as you can find.' His servants did so, bringing both the good and the bad as they returned. These guests filled the wedding hall, but when the king came in to see them, he saw a man who had no wedding clothes. 'Friend, how did you get in here without wedding clothes?' he wanted to know. The man was speechless. And the king said to those attending, 'Tie him up hand and foot and throw him outside into the darkness. In that place, there will be weeping and gnashing of teeth.' For many are called, but few are chosen."

[129]Elsewhere, the Pharisees were plotting how to trap him in his words. They sent some Pharisees and Herodians to him as spies, feigning sincerity, trying to trap him in his words so that they could report him to the power and authority of the governor.

They approached him and said, "Teacher, we know that you teach the truth about God's ways and you don't play

---

[128]Matthew 22:1-14
[129]Mark 12:13-27; Matthew 22:15-33; Luke 20:19-40

favorites since you're not influenced by looks. Now tell us what you think: Is it lawful to pay taxes to Caesar or not? Should we pay them or not?"

He could see right through their deceitfulness, and he said to them, "Why are you hypocrites testing me? Bring me a Roman coin and let me look at it."

They gave him one. "Whose likeness and inscription is this?" he asked.

"Caesar's," they said.

"Then give Caesar the things that belong to Caesar, and give God the things that are God's."

They had failed in front of everyone. They could not catch him in anything he said. Instead, they were silently marveling at his answer. Then they left.

That same day, some Sadducees came to him. (Sadducees don't believe anyone will ever be resurrected.) They asked him a question, "Teacher, Moses wrote for us that [130] *if a man's brother dies and leaves a wife, but leaves no child, the man must take the widow and raise up children for his brother.* Now there were seven brothers among us. The first got married and died without a child, and he left his wife to his brother. This second husband married her and died without a child. So did the third through seventh husbands, and none of them produced a child. Finally, the woman died. The question is this: In the resurrection when they rise again, whose wife will she be? For seven husbands all had her as a wife."

Jesus said to them, "See, that's where you went wrong because you don't understand the Scriptures or the power of God. The sons of this age marry and are given away in marriage. But those who are found worthy to get into the next age and are resurrected from the dead neither marry nor are given away in marriage. They can't die anymore because they are equal to angels and are sons of God, being sons of the resurrection. As far as the dead being raised, have you not

---

[130] Deuteronomy 25:5

133

read in the book of Moses, in the passage about the bush, how God spoke to him saying, [131]*I am the God of Abraham, and the God of Isaac, and the God of Jacob?* He is not God of the dead, but of the living, for all live to him. You are all very wrong."

The crowd heard all of this, and his teaching amazed them. Even some of the scribes answered, "Teacher, that was well-spoken." And they didn't dare ask him any more questions.

[132]Then the Pharisees heard that he had silenced the Sadducees, and they all got together. One of the scribes, a lawyer, came up and heard them arguing with one another and realizing that Jesus answered them so well, asked him a question to test him. "Teacher, which commandment in the Law is the most important?"

"The most important is, [133]*Hear, O Israel, the Lord our God, the Lord is one, and you shall love the Lord your God with all your heart and with all your soul and with all your mind and with all your strength.* This is the first and most important commandment. The second is like it: *You shall love your neighbor as yourself.* There is no other commandment greater than these. The Law and the Prophets depend on these two commandments."

"You are right, Teacher," said the scribe. "You spoke the truth when you said that he is one, and there is no other besides him, and to love him with all the heart and with all the understanding and with all the strength. You were right to say that to love one's neighbor as oneself is worth much more than all whole burnt offerings and sacrifices."

When Jesus heard his wise answer, he said to him, "You are not far from the kingdom of God." After that, no one dared ask him any more questions.

---

[131] Exodus 3:6
[132] Mark 12:28-34; Matthew 22:34-40
[133] Deuteronomy 6:5; Leviticus 19:18

[134]Later, as Jesus taught in the temple, he said, "What do you think about the Messiah? Whose son is he?"

"The son of David," they answered.

"How can the scribes say that the Messiah is the son of David?" he asked the gathering Pharisees. "David himself, in the Holy Spirit, calls him Lord, saying in the book of Psalms,

[135]*The Lord said to my Lord,*

sit at my right hand

until I put your enemies under your feet.

David himself calls him Lord. Then how is he his son?"

There were so many people, and while they were happy to listen to him, no one was able to answer a word in reply. From that day on, no one dared to ask him any more questions.

Jesus said to the crowds and to his disciples, "The scribes and the Pharisees sit on Moses' seat, but you should practice what they preach, not what they do because they don't practice what they preach. They devour widows' houses and pray long prayers only for show. They tie up heavy burdens that are hard to bear and lay them on people's shoulders, but they are not willing to lift a finger to help. They do everything in order to be seen by others. They will receive the greater condemnation because they like to walk around in long robes with longer tassels and make bigger boxes to put Scripture in and wear. They love the place of honor at feasts and the best seats in the synagogues and to be greeted properly in the marketplaces – being called 'rabbi' by others. But you shouldn't be called "rabbi," for you have one teacher, and that makes you all brothers. So don't call any man on Earth, "father." You have one Father – he is in Heaven. And don't let people call you 'teacher.' You have one teacher – the Messiah. The one who serves you will be the

---

[134]Mark 12:35-40; Matthew 22:41-23:36; Luke 20:41-47
[135]Psalm 110:1

greatest among you. Whoever exalts himself will be humbled, and whoever humbles himself will be exalted."

"Oh how terrible it will be for you scribes and Pharisees – you hypocrites! You slam the door to the kingdom of Heaven in people's faces. Not only do you not go in, but you stop others who want to go in."

"Oh how terrible it will be for you scribes and Pharisees – you hypocrites! You travel across land and sea to make a single convert, and when he converts, you make him twice as much a son of Hell as yourselves."

"Oh how terrible it will be for you, you blind guides, who say, 'If anyone swears by the temple, that's nothing, but if anyone swears by the gold of the temple, he must keep his promise.' You blind fools! Which is greater, the gold or the temple that makes the gold sacred? You also say, 'If anyone swears by the altar, that's nothing, but if anyone swears by the gift that's on the altar, then he must keep his promise.' You blind men! Which is greater, the gift or the altar that makes the gift sacred? Whoever swears by the altar swears by it and by everything on it, and whoever swears by the temple swears by it and by him who dwells in it, and whoever swears by Heaven swears by the throne of God and by him who sits on it."

"How terrible it will be for you scribes and Pharisees – you hypocrites! You tithe mint and dill and cumin, but you neglect the more important matters of the Law like justice and mercy and faithfulness. You should have done these, without neglecting the others. You blind guides, straining out a gnat and swallowing a camel!"

"How terrible it will be for you scribes and Pharisees – you hypocrites! You clean the outside of the cup and the plate, but inside you are full of greed and selfishness. You blind Pharisee! First, clean the inside of the cup and the plate, then the outside can be clean."

"How terrible it will be for you scribes and Pharisees – you hypocrites! You are like tombs painted white. On the outside they are beautiful, but inside they are full of dead men's bones and filth. You are the same way. You look righteous to others on the outside, but inside you are full of hypocrisy and lawlessness."

"Oh how terrible it will be for you scribes and Pharisees – you hypocrites! You build the prophets' tombs and decorate the monuments of the righteous, saying, 'If we had lived in the days of our ancestors, we would not have taken part with them in killing the prophets.' So you testify against yourselves that you are sons of those who murdered the prophets. Go on and finish what your fathers started. You snakes, you sons of vipers, how will you escape being condemned to Hell? Therefore, I send you prophets and wise men and scribes, some of whom you will kill and crucify, and some you will beat in your synagogues and persecute from town to town, so that all the righteous blood shed on Earth may fall on you, from the blood of innocent Abel to the blood of Zechariah the son of Barachiah whom you murdered between the sanctuary and the altar. Truly I say to you, all these things will fall on this generation."

[136]Later, he sat down opposite the treasury and watched the people putting money into the offering box. Many rich people put in large amounts, and a poor widow came and put in two small copper coins, which make a penny.

Then he called his disciples and said to them, "The truth is – this poor widow has put in more than anyone contributing to the offering box. That's because they all gave out of their abundance, but she gave out of her poverty by putting in everything she had – all she had to live on."

[137]As he left the temple and was walking away, one of his disciples said to him, "Look teacher, what wonderful stones and what wonderful buildings!"

Jesus replied, "Do you see these grand buildings? Not one stone will be left on another that won't be torn down."

---

[136]Mark 12:41-44; Luke 21:1-4
[137]Mark 13:1-37; Matthew 24:1-44; Luke 21:5-36

Then as he sat on the Mount of Olives, opposite the temple, Peter, James, John, and Andrew asked him privately, "Teacher, tell us, when will all this happen, and what will be the sign when all these things are about to take place? And what will be the sign of your coming and the close of the age?"

"See that no one deceives you on this," Jesus answered. "Many will come in my name, saying, 'I am the Messiah! I am the one! The time is at hand!' They will mislead many. Don't go after them, and when you hear of wars and rumors of wars, don't let that shake you. All this must take place, but that's not the end. For nation will rise against nation and kingdom against kingdom. There will be earthquakes in different places, along with famines and pestilences. There will be terrible things and great signs from Heaven. But all this is only the beginning of the birth pains."

"So be on your guard. Before all this, they will take hold of you and persecute you. They will deliver you over to councils and prisons. You will be beaten in synagogues, and you will stand before governors and kings for my name's sake to be a witness to them. Then many will fall away and betray and hate each other. But when they take you to trial and deliver you over, don't be anxious ahead of time about what you are to say – just say whatever you are given at that time because I will give you the words and the wisdom, which none of your adversaries will be able to stand against or contradict. It will not be you speaking but the Holy Spirit."

Brother will deliver brother over to death, and a father will give up his child, and children will rise against parents and have them put to death. You will be delivered up by relatives and friends, and some of you they will put to death. You will be hated by all nations for my name's sake, but not a hair of your head will perish, and the one who endures to the end will be saved. Many false prophets will rise up and deceive many. And because lawlessness will be multiplied, the love of many will grow cold. Still, this gospel of the kingdom will be proclaimed throughout the whole world as a testimony to all people groups, and then the end will come."

"But when you see the abomination of desolation, spoken of by the prophet [138]Daniel, standing in the holy place where it should not be (the reader needs to understand this) and when you see Jerusalem surrounded by armies, then know that its desolation is close at hand. Anyone in Judea should escape to the mountains. Anyone on the housetop should not go get anything out of his house before he leaves. The same goes for anyone in the field – don't go back to get your coat. Those who are in the city – leave immediately, and those who are out in the country should not go into the city before they leave. These are days of vengeance that will fulfill all that is written. Oh how terrible for women who are pregnant and for those who are nursing babies in those days! Pray that your escape won't be in winter or on a Sabbath because tribulation in those days will be the worst it has ever been, from the beginning of all God created until now and forever. There will be overwhelming distress on the earth and wrath against this people. They will be cut down by the sword and led captive among all nations, and Jerusalem will be trampled underfoot by the Gentiles until the Gentile era is fulfilled. If the Lord had not limited these days, no human being would be saved, but for the sake of his chosen ones, he shortened the days."

If anyone says to you, 'Look, here is the Messiah!' or 'Look, there he is!' Don't believe it. False messiahs and false prophets will appear and perform great signs and wonders to lead even the chosen ones astray – if that's possible. Be on high alert. I have told you all of this ahead of time. If they say to you, 'Look, he is in the wilderness,' don't go. If they say, 'Look, he's in a secret room,' don't believe it. The real coming of the Son of Man will be like lightning striking from the east,

---

[138] Daniel 9:27

lighting up the sky as far as the west. Wherever the dead are, that's where the vultures will gather."

"During that time and after that tribulation there will be signs. The sun will be darkened, and the moon won't shine, and the stars will be falling from Heaven because the powers in the heavens will be shaken. The nations on Earth will be distressed and perplexed at how the sea roars with the waves. People will faint with fear and the foreboding of what's coming on the world. Then the sign of the Son of Man will appear in heaven, and all the tribes of the earth will mourn, and they will see the Son of Man coming on the clouds of heaven with power and great glory."

"When all these things start happening, sit up and pay attention because your redemption is drawing near. He will send out the angels with a loud trumpet call, and they will gather his chosen ones from the four winds, from the ends of the earth to the ends of the heavens."

Then he told them a parable: "Look at the fig tree, and all the trees, and learn this lesson: As soon as its branch becomes tender and puts out its leaves, you see it and you know that summer's almost here. In the same way, when you see these things taking place, you know that the kingdom of God is near, and you know that he is near, approaching the gates. Truly I declare to you, this generation will not pass away until all these things take place. Heaven and Earth will pass away, but my words will not pass away. However, concerning that day or that hour, no one knows, not the angels in Heaven, not even the Son – only the Father knows that."

"Be on guard. Stay awake. Because you don't know when the time will come. It's like a man going on a journey. When he leaves home, he puts his servants in charge, giving each his work to do and commanding the doorkeeper to stay awake. Therefore, stay awake, for you don't know when the master of the house will come – in the evening, or at midnight, or when the cock crows, or in the morning. You don't want him to show up suddenly and find you asleep. What I say to you, I say to everyone: Stay awake."

He went on to say, "The way it was in the days of Noah is how it will be when the Son of Man comes. In those days before the flood, they were eating and drinking, marrying and giving in marriage, until the day Noah entered the ark. They were oblivious until the flood came and swept them all away. That's how it will be when the Son of Man comes. Two men will be in the field – one will be taken and one left. Two women will be grinding at the mill – one will be taken and one left. Therefore, stay awake because you don't know what day your Lord is coming. But know this, if the master of the house had known the time of night the thief was coming, he would have stayed awake and would not have let his house be broken into."

"Be very careful or your hearts will get weighed down with wasted living and drunkenness and the problems of life. Then, the day the Messiah returns will spring on you like a trap. Everyone who lives on Earth will experience it – so don't ever go to sleep. Keep praying for the strength to escape everything that will happen and for the strength to stand before the Son of Man. He will come when you least expect it, so you better be ready."

[139]He went on to say, "Who will be the faithful and wise servant, the one his master appoints to lead his household, who feeds them at the right time? When the master comes, imagine how blessed that servant will be. The truth is – he will put him in leadership over all he owns. But if that wicked servant says to himself, 'My master is going to be late,' and starts abusing his fellow servants and hanging out with drunkards, the servant's master will show up unexpectedly on a day and time he does not know and will tear him to pieces and put him with the hypocrites. In that place there will be weeping and gnashing of teeth."

---

[139]Matthew 24:45-25:46

"At that time, the kingdom of Heaven will be like ten virgins who took their lamps and went to meet the bridegroom. Five of them were foolish and five were wise because the foolish took no oil for their lamps, but the wise did."

"When the bridegroom was delayed, they all became tired and went to sleep. But at midnight someone shouted, 'The bridegroom is here! Come meet him.' All the virgins got up and trimmed their lamps and the foolish said to the wise, 'Give us some of your oil; our lamps are going out.' But the wise answered, 'There's not enough for all of us. You go buy some from the store.' While they were going to buy the oil, the bridegroom came, and those who were ready went in with him to the marriage supper, and the door was shut. Later, the other virgins arrived saying, 'Lord, lord, open up for us,' but he answered, 'The truth is – I don't know you.' So you better pay attention – you don't know the day or the time."

"It's kind of like a man going on a journey who called his servants and put them in charge of his property. To one he gave five talents, to another two, and to another one. He distributed the money according to their ability. Then he left. The servant who had received the five talents immediately went and did business with them, and he made five more talents. The servant with two talents did the same and made two more talents. However, the servant who had received the one talent went and buried it in the ground and hid his master's money. A long time passed before the master of those servants returned and settled accounts with them. The one who had received the five talents came bringing five more talents saying, 'Master, you left me with five talents. Here, I've made five more talents.' His master said, 'Well done, good and faithful servant. You've been faithful over a little. I'll put you in charge of much more. Go and enter into the joy of your master.' Next, the one who had the two talents came up, saying, 'Master, you left me with two talents. Here, I've made two more talents.' His master said to him, 'Well done, good and faithful servant. You've been faithful over a little. I'll put you in charge of much more. Go and enter into the joy of your master.' Then the one who had received the one talent came forward, saying, 'Master, I knew you to be a hard man. You reap where you don't sow and gather where you planted no seed, so I was afraid, and I went and hid your talent in the ground. Here, you can have it back.' His master told him, 'You wicked and lazy servant! You knew that I reap where I have not sown and gather where I planted no seed. You should have invested my money at the bank, so that when I returned, I would have received my money with interest. Take that talent from him and give it to the servant who has the ten talents because more will be given to everyone who has some already – and he will have so much more. On the other hand, the one who made nothing, even what he has will be taken away from him. And throw that worthless servant into the darkness outside. In that place there will be weeping and gnashing of teeth.'"

"When the Son of Man comes in his glory, and all the angels with him, then he will sit on his glorious throne. All the nations will be gathered before him, and he will separate people one from another like a shepherd separates the sheep from the goats. He will place the sheep on his right and the goats on the left. Then the king will say to those on his right, 'Come, you who are blessed by my father – inherit the kingdom prepared for you from the world's beginning. For when I was hungry, you gave me food. When I was thirsty, you gave me a drink. When I was a stranger, you welcomed me. When I was naked, you clothed me. When I was sick, you visited me. When I was in prison, you came to see me.' Then the righteous will answer him, 'Lord, when did we see you hungry and feed you or thirsty and give you a drink? When did we see you a stranger and welcome you or naked and clothe you? And when did we see you sick or in prison and come visit you?' And the king will answer them, 'To tell you the truth, when you did it to one of the least of my brothers, you did it to me.'"

"Then he will say to those on his left, 'Get away from me, you cursed people, into the fire of the ages prepared for the Devil and his angels. I was hungry and you gave me nothing to eat. I was thirsty and you gave me nothing to drink. I was a stranger and you did not welcome me, naked and you did not clothe me, sick and in prison and you did not visit me.' Then they will also answer, 'Lord, when did we see you hungry or thirsty or a stranger or naked or sick or in prison and did not help you?' And he will answer them, 'To tell you the truth, when you did not do it to one of the least of these, you did not do it to me.' Now these will go away into the punishment for the age, but the righteous will go into the life of the coming age."

[140]Every day Jesus was teaching in the temple, but at night he went and stayed on the mount called Olivet. Early in the morning, all the people came to hear him in the temple. When Jesus had finished all he had to say, it was two days before the Passover and the Feast of Unleavened Bread. Jesus said to his disciples, "You know that Passover is coming in two days, and the Son of Man will be handed over to be crucified."

The chief priests, scribes, and elders of the people had gathered in the palace of Caiaphas, the high priest, and plotted together to take Jesus by surprise and kill him. But because they feared the people, they said, "Not during the feast since it could cause a riot."

Then Satan entered into Judas called Iscariot, who was one of the twelve. He went to the chief priests and officers so he could betray Jesus to them. He asked, "What will you give me if I give him up to you?"

They were excited to hear this and promised to give him thirty pieces of silver. He made the deal. And from that moment, he looked for an opportunity to betray him to them

---

[140]Mark 14:1-2,10-16; Matthew 26:1-5,14-19;
Luke 21:37-22:13

when the crowd was not around. On the first day of Unleavened Bread, when the Passover lamb had to be sacrificed, the disciples asked Jesus, "Where do you want us to go and prepare for you to eat the Passover?"

He sent Peter and John after he told them, "Go into the city and a man will meet you carrying a jar of water. Follow him, and wherever he enters, say to the master of the house, 'The Teacher says it's his time now.' He says, 'I will keep the Passover at your house. Where is my guest room where I may eat the Passover with my disciples?' Then he will show you a large upper room furnished and ready where you can prepare for us." So the disciples headed into the city and found things just as he had told them, and they prepared the Passover.

The Last Supper

[141]Jesus knew before the Passover Feast that his time had come to leave this world and go to the Father. And loving his own who were in the world, he loved them to the very end.

When the hour came and it was evening, he reclined with his apostles at the table.

They began to argue over which one of them should be regarded as the greatest. Jesus spoke up, "The kings of the Gentiles rule as lords over them, but call themselves philanthropists. It can't be that way with you. Instead, let the greatest among you become as the youngest, and let the leader become the one who serves. Which one is greater, the one who reclines at the table or the one who serves? The one who reclines, right? But I am among you as the one who serves. Also, I have looked forward to eating this Passover with you before I suffer."

Now the Devil had already worked in the heart of Simon's son, Judas Iscariot, and he was ready to betray Jesus. Jesus also knew that the Father had given all things into his hands, and that he had come from and was going back to God. Afterward, during supper, Jesus got up and took off his outer clothing and tied a towel around his waist. He poured water into a large bowl and began to wash the disciples' feet and wipe them with the towel wrapped around him. He came to Simon Peter who said to him, "Lord, are you about to wash my feet?"

"You don't understand what I'm doing now, but you will later," Jesus replied.

"You will never wash my feet!" Peter declared.

"If I don't wash you," said Jesus, "you're not a part of this with me."

---

[141]Mark 14:17-25; Matthew 26:20-29; Luke 22:14-30; John 13:1-32

Simon Peter said, "Lord, don't just wash my feet then, wash my hands and my head too!"

"The one who has bathed," said Jesus, "doesn't need to wash his body, just his feet, since he is completely clean. And you are clean, but not every one of you."

He knew who would betray him. That's why he said, "Not every one of you is clean."

After he had washed their feet, he put on his outer clothing and returned to his place. He said to them, "Do you understand what I have done to you? You call me "Teacher" and "Lord," and you are right because I am. So if your Lord and Teacher washed your feet, you should also wash one another's feet. This is the example I am giving you that you should do the same as I have done to you. The truth I tell you is this: a servant is not greater than his master, and a messenger is not greater than the one who sent him. If you know these things, you're blessed if you do them. I know the ones I have chosen. I'm not speaking of all of you. Yet the Scripture will be fulfilled: [142]*He who ate my bread has lifted his heel against me.* I'm telling you this before it takes place so that when it does, you may believe that I am. What I tell you is true – whoever receives the one I send receives me, and whoever receives me receives the one who sent me."

After saying these things, Jesus was troubled in his spirit, and he shared this testimony: "The truth is – one of you will betray me, and his hand is on the table eating with me."

The disciples looked at one another, unsure of who he was talking about, and they began to question each other as to which one of them it could be. They even became sad and started asking, one after another, "Lord is it me?"

The disciple Jesus loved was reclining close to Jesus at the table, so Simon Peter motioned to him to ask Jesus who he was referring to. That disciple leaned back against Jesus and asked him, "Lord, who is it?"

---

[142] Psalm 41:9

"It's the one I will give this piece of bread to after I have dipped it."

When he had dipped the piece, he gave it to Judas, the son of Simon Iscariot. Jesus said, "He who has dipped his hand in the dish with me will betray me. The Son of Man submits to what is written about him, but how terrible for that man who betrays the Son of Man. It would have been better for him if he had never been born."

"Am I the one, Rabbi?" asked Judas, the betrayer.

"You said it," he replied.

And he took the morsel from Jesus. Then Satan entered into him. Jesus said, "Do what you are going to do – quickly."

No one at the table knew what he meant. Since Judas was the treasure, some thought that Jesus was telling him to buy what they needed for the feast or to give something to the poor. So after receiving the piece of bread, he left immediately into the night.

After he left, Jesus said, "Now the Son of Man is glorified, and God is glorified in him. If God is glorified in him, God will also bring him glory in himself at the same time."

"You are the ones who have stuck by me through my trials, and I am giving you a kingdom, just as my Father gave it to me, so that you may eat and drink at my table in my kingdom and sit on thrones judging the twelve tribes of Israel."

As they were eating, Jesus took bread, and after blessing it, he broke it and gave it to them. He said, "Take this and eat it. This is my body which is given for you. Do this and remember me."

Then he took a cup and gave thanks and gave it to them saying, "Take this, and give some to each one of you."

He told them, "All of you drink it. This is my blood of the covenant which is poured out for many, so their sins will be forgiven. I can also tell you that I will not drink this fruit of the vine again until that day when we drink it together in my Father's kingdom."

And they all drank it.

[143]Then Jesus said, "Little children, I'm only going to be with you a short while. You will look for me, and I'll tell you like I told the Jews, 'You cannot go where I am going.'"

"And I'm giving you a new commandment. I want you to love each other. I want you to love each other the same way I have loved you. That's how all people will know that you are my followers – if you love each other."

"Lord, where are you going?" Simon Peter asked.

"Where I'm going you can't follow right now. But later you will."

"Lord, why can't I follow you now? I will lay down my life for you," Peter declared.

"Will you lay down your life for me? The truth is – before the rooster crows you will have denied me three times."

"Don't stress about all this – believe in God and trust me. There are many rooms in my Father's house. If not, I wouldn't tell you that I go to prepare a place for you. Now if I go and prepare a place for you, I will come back and take you to be with me, so that you will be where I am – and you know how to get there."

"Lord, we don't even know where you're going," said Thomas. "How can we know the way?"

"I am the way and the truth and the life," explained Jesus. "No one comes to the Father unless they come through me. If you had known me, you would have known my Father too. From now on, you do know him, and you have seen him."

Philip implored him, "Lord, just show us the Father, and that will be enough for us."

"Philip, have I been with you this long, and you still don't know me? Whoever has seen me has seen the Father. How can you say, 'Show us the Father?' Do you not believe

---

[143]John 13:33-14:31

that I am in the Father and the Father is in me? The words that I say to you, I don't speak on my own authority, but the Father who dwells in me does his works. Believe me that I am in the Father and the Father is in me. Otherwise, believe on account of the works you have seen me do."

"The truth is – whoever believes in me will do the works that I do, and he will do even greater works than I do because I am going to the Father. Whatever you ask in my name, I will do it, so that the Father may be glorified in the Son. If you ask me anything in my name, I will do it."

"If you love me, you will keep my commandments, and I will ask the Father and he will give you another Helper. The Helper, or the Spirit of truth, will be with you forever. The world cannot receive him because it doesn't see him or know him. You do know him because he lives with you and will be in you."

"I will not leave you as orphans. I will come to you. In a little while, the world will not see me anymore, but you will. Because I live, you will live. When that day comes, you will know that I am in my Father, and you are in me, and I am in you. Whoever has my commandments and keeps them, he is the one who loves me, and the one who loves me will be loved by my Father, and I will love him and reveal myself to him."

Judas (not Iscariot) said to him, "Lord, how or why will you reveal yourself to us and not to the world?"

"If anyone loves me, he will do what I say, and my Father will love him, and we will come to him and make our home with him. Whoever does not love me, does not do what I say, and what you hear me saying is not from me but from the Father who sent me."

"I have told you all these things while I'm still with you. But the Helper, the Holy Spirit, whom the Father will send in my name, will teach you all things and cause you to remember everything I've said to you. I leave you peace. Not the peace the world can give. Instead, I give you my kind of peace."

"Don't let your hearts be troubled, and don't let your hearts be afraid. You heard me tell you, 'I am going away, and I will come back to you.' If you loved me, this would have excited you that I am going to the Father because the Father is greater than I am. I've told you all this before it happens so that when it does happen you can believe. I will not say much more to you because the ruler of this world is coming. He has no hold on me, but I do as the Father has commanded me so that the world may know that I love the Father. Now get up and let's leave from here."

[144]"I am the true vine and my Father is the gardener. Every branch of mine that does not bear fruit, he takes away. And he prunes every branch that does bear fruit, so it can bear more fruit. You are already clean because of the word that I've spoken to you. Be at home in me and live in me, and I will be at home in you and live in you. Just as the branch cannot produce fruit by itself unless it lives in the vine, neither can you unless you abide in me. I am the vine and you are the branches. Whoever is at home in me and lives in me, and I in him, he will be the one who bears much fruit. Apart from me you can do nothing. If anyone does not abide in me, he is thrown away like a branch and withers, and the branches are gathered, thrown into the fire, and burned. If you are at home in and live in me, and my words are at home in and live in you, ask for anything you want and it will be done for you. When you produce much fruit, which proves you are my disciples, my Father is glorified. I have loved you like the Father has loved me."

"So be at home in and live in my love. If you keep my commandments, you will abide in my love just as I have kept my Father's commandments and abide in his love. I say all these things to you so that my joy may be in you, and that your joy may be filled to the top."

---

[144]John 15:1-27

"This is my commandment: love one another like I have loved you. No one can top this love – the love when someone lays down his life for his friends. You are my friends if you do what I command you. I don't call you servants anymore because the servant does not know what his master is doing. Instead, I have called you friends since I reveal to you all I have heard from my Father. You did not choose me, but I chose you. And I appointed you, that you would go and bear fruit, and that your fruit should always stay fresh, so that whatever you ask the Father in my name, he will give it to you. I demand these things from you so you will love one another."

"If the world hates you, remember that it hated me before it hated you. The world would love you as its own if you were part of it, but because I chose you out of the world, you are not of it. Therefore, the world hates you. Remember what I said to you: 'A servant is not greater than his master.' If they persecuted me, they will also persecute you. If they did what I said, they will do what you say. So they are going to do what they do to you because of my name since they don't know the one who sent me. They wouldn't be guilty of sin if I had not come and spoken to them, but now they have no excuse for their sin. Whoever hates me hates my Father also. They wouldn't be guilty of sin if I had not done the works that no one else did among them, but now they have seen and hated both me and my Father. Still, the word that is written in their Law must be fulfilled: [145]*They hated me for no reason.*"

"I will send you the Helper, who is the Spirit of truth. He comes from the Father, and when he gets here, he will bear witness about me. You will also bear witness because you have been with me from the beginning."

---

[145] Psalm 35:19; 69:4

[146]"I tell you all this to keep you from falling away. They will kick you out of the synagogues. In fact, the time is coming when whoever kills you will think he's doing it for God. And they will do these things because they have not known the Father or me. Yet, I've said these things to you so that when their time comes, you will remember what I told you about them."

"I didn't tell you all this from the beginning because I was with you then. But now I am going to the one who sent me, and none of you asks me, 'Where are you going?' However, because I told you these things, your hearts have become filled with sadness. The truth is – it will be better for you that I leave because if I don't, the Helper will not come. But if I go, I will send him to you. And when he comes, he will convict the world of sin and righteousness and judgment. He will convict of sin because they don't believe in me, of righteousness because I go to the Father and you won't see me any longer, and of judgment because the ruler of this world is judged."

"I still have so much to say to you, but you can't handle it all now. When the Spirit of truth comes, he will guide you into all the truth. He will not speak on his own authority, but whatever he hears he will speak, and he will announce to you the things that are to come. He will glorify me by taking what is mine and declaring it to you. All that the Father has is mine. That's why I said that he will take what is mine and announce it to you."

"In a little while you won't see me any longer, and then a little later you will see me."

Some of his disciples said to one another, "What is he talking about, 'In a little while you won't see me, and then a little later you will see me,' and 'Because I am going to the Father'?"

---

[146]John 16:1-33

They were repeating, "What does he mean by 'a little while'? We don't know what he's talking about."

Jesus knew that they wanted to ask him and he said, "Is this what you are asking yourselves, what I meant by saying, 'In a little while you won't see me, and then a little later you will see me'? The truth is – you will weep and lament, but the world will shout for joy. You will be very sad, but your sorrow will turn into joy. When a woman is giving birth she is sad because 'It's time!' but once she has delivered the baby, the joy of bringing a person into the world makes her forget the pain. In the same way, you are sad now, but I will see you again and your hearts will jump for joy, and no one will be able to take your joy away from you. In that day, you won't ask me for anything. The truth is – whatever you ask from the Father in my name, he will give it to you. Until now you haven't asked for anything in my name. Ask, and you will receive so that your joy may be full."

"I've used figures of speech to tell you all these things. The hour is coming when I won't use figures of speech but will tell you plainly about the Father. When that day comes, you will ask in my name, but I'm not saying that I will ask the Father on your behalf, for the Father himself loves you because you have loved me and have believed that I came from God. I came into the world from the Father, and now I am leaving the world and going back to the Father."

His disciples said, "Ok, now you are speaking plainly and not figuratively! Now we understand that you know all things and do not need anyone to question you. This is why we believe that you came from God."

Jesus answered them, "Oh now you believe? Listen, the hour is coming – actually it's here – when you will be scattered and go home, leaving me all alone. Although, I'm not alone – the Father is with me. I have told you these things so you can have peace in me. In the world you will have tribulation, but hold on to your heart – I have overcome the world."

[147]After Jesus spoke these words, he looked up to Heaven and said, "Father, it is time. Glorify your Son so that the Son may glorify you since you have given him authority over all flesh to give the life of the ages to all you have given him. This is the life of the ages: to know you, the only true God and Jesus Christ – the one you have sent. I glorified you on Earth by accomplishing the work you gave me to do. And now Father, glorify me in your own presence with the glory I had with you before the world existed."

"I have revealed your name to the people you gave me out of the world. They were yours, and you gave them to me, and they have kept your word. Now they know that everything you have given me is from you. I have given them the words that you gave me, and they took it all in and have come to know the truth – that I came from you. They believe that you sent me."

"I am praying for them. I am not praying for the world but for those you have given me because they are yours. All mine are yours and yours are mine, and they are my glory. I am no longer in the world, but they are, and I am coming to you."

"Holy Father, keep them in your name – the name you have given me. I want them to be one, like we are. While I was with them, I kept them in your name – the one you gave me. I've guarded them without losing a single one, except the son of destruction, that the Scripture might be fulfilled. But now I am coming to you, and I speak these things in the world so that my kind of joy will be their kind of joy. I've given them your word, and the world has hated them because they are not of this world, just as I am not of the world. I'm not asking you to take them out of the world, but to keep them from the evil one. Like me, they are not of the world. Make them holy in the truth – your word is truth. You sent me into the world, and I have sent them into the world. And

---

[147]John 17:1-26

155

for them I dedicate myself that they also may be made holy in truth."

"I'm not asking for these only, but for all who will believe in me through their word. I'm asking that they all be one, as you, Father, are in me and I in you, that they also may be in us, so the world can believe that you sent me. I gave them the glory you gave me that they may be one even as we are one – I in them and you in me that they may become perfectly one. This way the world will know that you sent me and loved them just like you loved me."

Father, I want this too: for all the ones you've given me to be with me where I am. I want them to see my glory that you've given me because you loved me before the foundation of the world. Righteous Father, even though the world does not know you, I know you, and these know that you have sent me. I revealed your name to them, and I will continue to make it known, so that the love you loved me with may be in them, and I in them."

From the Garden to Golgotha

[148]After they sang a hymn, they left and crossed the Kidron Valley and arrived as they usually did at the Mount of Olives. Then Jesus said to them, "You will all desert me, just like it's written, [149]*I will strike the shepherd and the sheep of the flock will be scattered.* And after I am raised up, I will go to Galilee ahead of you."

Peter said to him, "They might all fall away because of you, but I won't."

"Simon, Simon, can't you see, Satan has demanded to have you so he can sift you like wheat. But I've been praying that your faith won't give up. So when you have repented, go strengthen your brothers."

"Lord, I'm ready to go to prison and death with you," Peter said.

"I tell you Peter, before the rooster crows today you will have denied three times that you even know me. In fact, I tell you that tonight before the rooster crows twice, you'll deny me three times."

Yet he demanded all the more, "Even if I have to die with you, I will not deny you!" And all the disciples echoed this.

[150]Then he said to them, "When I sent you out with no wallet or backpack or sandals, did you need anything?"

"Not a thing," they said.

"Now," he said, "let the one who has a wallet take it along with his backpack. Anyone without a sword should sell his coat and buy one because this Scripture must be fulfilled

---

[148] Mark 14:26-31; Matthew 26:30-35; Luke 22:31-34
[149] Zechariah 13:7
[150] Mark 14:32-42; Matthew 26:36-46; Luke 22:35-46; John 18:1

in me: [151]*And he was counted among the transgressors.* What is written about me will happen."

And they said, "Lord, look! Here are two swords."

Jesus ended the conversation by saying, "That's enough of this."

They came to a garden of olive trees called Gethsemane. "Sit here," said Jesus, "while I go over there and pray. And pray that you don't fall into temptation."

Then he took Peter and the two sons of Zebedee with him, James and John, and as deep stress and trouble came over him he said, "My soul is in so much pain I could die. Stay here and stay awake with me."

He went on a little farther, about a stone's throw, where he knelt down on the ground and fell on his face praying, "Dad, Father, you can do anything you choose. If there is another way, and you want to, take this cup away from me! Most of all, do your will, not mine."

When he went back to the disciples, he found them sleeping and he said to Peter, "Simon, are you asleep? You mean you couldn't stay awake with me for one hour? Indeed, the spirit is willing, but the flesh is weak. Stay awake now and pray that you don't fall into temptation."

He went and prayed for the second time saying the same words: "My Father, if this can't be done unless I drink it, then your will be done."

When he came back, he found them sleeping again. They were exhausted and didn't know what to say to him.

So he left them again and went and prayed for the third time, saying the same words, and an angel from Heaven appeared to him and was strengthening him. He was in agony and prayed even harder as his sweat became like great drops of blood falling to the ground.

After this, he came to the disciples and said, "Are you still sleeping? That's enough, you can do that later. Now it's

---

[151] Isaiah 53:12

time and the Son of Man is being betrayed into the hands of sinners. Get up and let's go. Look – my betrayer is already here."

[152]Immediately, while he was still speaking, Judas arrived. Being one of the twelve, Judas knew the place because Jesus often met there with his disciples. So he gathered a band of soldiers and some officers from the chief priests and the Pharisees, along with scribes and elders of the people. They all came carrying lanterns and torches and armed with swords and clubs.

The betrayer had given them a sign saying, "The one I will kiss is the man. Arrest him."

He walked straight to Jesus and said, "Hello, Rabbi!" And he kissed him.

"Judas. My friend. Do what you came to do. But would you betray the Son of Man with a kiss?"

Jesus knew all that would happen. Still, he approached them and asked, "Who are you looking for?"

"Jesus of Nazareth."

"I am," said Jesus.

When he said, "I am," they backed up and fell to the ground, including Judas who had just betrayed him and was standing with them.

"Who are you looking for?" he repeated.

"Jesus of Nazareth," they said again.

"I told you that I am. So if I'm the one you want, let these men go."

He said this to fulfill what he had said: "I didn't lose even one of those you gave me."

Those around him saw what was happening and asked, "Lord, should we use our swords?" as Simon Peter drew his and struck Malchus, the servant of the high priest, cutting off his right ear.

---

[152] Mark 14:43-52; Matthew 27:47-56; Luke 22:47-53; John 18:2-11

"No more of this!" Jesus demanded. "Put your sword into its sheath. Shouldn't I drink the cup that the Father has given me? For all who use the sword will die by the sword. Don't you know that I can ask my Father, and right now he will send me more than 72,000 angels? But how would that accomplish the Scriptures? They must be fulfilled." And he touched Malchus' ear and healed him.

Jesus said to the chief priests, temple officers, and elders amassed against him, "What am I, a robber, that you have all these swords and clubs? You didn't lay a hand on me when I was with you day after day in the temple. But this is your time and the power of darkness."

Then all the disciples left him and ran away. However, one young man was following him wearing only a linen cloth. They grabbed him, but he left the linen cloth and ran away naked.

[153]The soldiers, captain, and Jewish officers bound and arrested Jesus. First they took him to Annas, Caiaphas' father-in-law, who was high priest that year. Remember, Caiaphas had advised the Jews that it would be best to have just one man die for the people.

In the distance, Simon Peter followed Jesus as did another disciple. Because that disciple knew the high priest, he was let in with Jesus to the high priest's court, while Peter stood outside the door. Peter got in after the other disciple spoke to the servant girl who kept watch at the door.

It was cold. The guards started a charcoal fire in the middle of the courtyard and sat down together. Peter sat down with them trying to get warm by the fire. He wondered how this would end.

Elsewhere, the high priest questioned Jesus about his disciples and his teaching. Jesus answered, "I have spoken

---

[153] Mark 14:54,66-72; Matthew 26:58,69-75;
Luke 22:54-65; John 18:12-27

openly to the world. I always taught in synagogues and in the temple where all Jews come together. I say nothing in secret; so why ask me? Ask those who have heard me. They know what I said."

After Jesus spoke these things, one of the officers standing by slapped him and said, "Is that how you answer the high priest?"

"If I said something wrong, confront what is wrong, but if what I said is right, why hit me?"

Then Annas sent him bound to Caiaphas, the high priest.

Meanwhile, Peter was seated below in the courtyard, and a servant girl of the high priest stared at him as he sat in the light. She said, "This man was with the Nazarene Jesus, you know – the Galilean."

"You're not one of his disciples are you?" the others wondered.

"Woman, not me. I don't even know what you all are talking about," Peter said in denial as he headed for the gateway. Then a rooster crowed.

A little later, that servant girl and another servant girl saw him. They said to those standing around, "He's one of them. This man was with Jesus of Nazareth."

"Yeah, you are one of them," said another.

"No sir, I'm not," he denied with an oath. "I don't know the man."

About an hour passed, and bystanders insisted, "We know for sure this man was with him, and we can tell you're a Galilean by the way you talk!"

One of the high priest's servants, who was a relative of the man whose ear Peter had cut off, asked, "Didn't I see you in the garden with him?"

"Man, I don't know what you're talking about!" Peter argued, defending himself by calling for a curse if he were lying. He finished and swore, "I DO NOT KNOW THAT MAN!"

That very moment the rooster crowed the second time. The Lord turned and looked at Peter. Peter remembered,

161

"Before the rooster crows twice, you will deny me three times."

He broke down. Cried bitterly. And ran away.

[154]Then day came. All the chief priests, elders, and scribes came together, as the whole Council was seeking false witnesses against Jesus in order to put him to death, but they couldn't find any. They actually got many false witnesses to come forward, but their stories didn't agree. Finally, two came forward and declared, "This man said, 'I can destroy God's temple that was man-made and rebuild another in three days that is not man-made.'" However, they couldn't even get their story straight on this. So the high priest stood up and said, "Don't you have anything to say? What are these men accusing you of?"

Jesus didn't say a word.

"I command you by the living God," the high priest continued to demand, "tell us if you are the Messiah, Son of the Blessed, the Son of God!"

"You won't believe me if I tell you," replied Jesus. "And you won't answer if I ask you. So...you say that I am."

Again they pressed him, "If you are the Messiah, tell us!"

"I am," he said, "but from now on I tell you, you will see [155]*the Son of Man seated at the right hand of power and coming on the clouds of Heaven.*"

"He just blasphemed!" the high priest declared as he tore his robes. "What more do we need with witnesses? You all heard his blasphemy. What is your judgment?"

"We have heard it ourselves from his own lips," they all agreed. "He deserves death!"

At this point, some began to spit in his face and hit him. Guards punched him, and others blindfolded him and slapped him, saying, "Prophesy for us, you Messiah! Who hit

---

[154] Mark 14:53,55-65; Matthew 26:57-68; Luke 22:63-71
[155] Psalm 110:1; Daniel 7:13

you?" And they kept at him, mocking and blaspheming him as they beat him.

[156]As it all progressed, Judas, his betrayer, realized that Jesus was condemned, and he changed his mind and took the thirty pieces of silver back to the chief priests and the elders. "I have sinned by betraying innocent blood," he told them.

"What do we care?" they said. "You deal with that yourself."

Judas threw the pieces of silver into the temple, left, and went and hanged himself.

The chief priests took the pieces of silver and said, "It's against the Law to put this into the treasury since its blood money." They talked it over and used the money to buy the potter's field as a burial place for strangers. To this day, they call that field the Field of Blood. This fulfilled the words spoken by the prophet Jeremiah: [157]*And they took the thirty pieces of silver, the purchase price set on him by some of the sons of Israel, and they gave them for the potter's field as the Lord directed me.*

[158]And the whole company got up, bound him, and led Jesus from the house of Caiaphas to Governor Pilate's headquarters. It was early morning. The Jews didn't enter the governor's headquarters because they wanted to remain undefiled in order to eat the Passover. Pilate went outside to them and asked, "What accusation do you bring against this man?"

"We wouldn't be here if this man weren't doing evil."

"Then you take him and judge him by your own law," Pilate retorted.

---

[156] Matthew 27:3-10
[157] Zechariah 11:12
[158] Mark 15:1-20; Matthew 27:1,11-31; Luke 23:1-25; John 18:33-19:16

But they reminded Pilate, "It is against the law for us to put anyone to death." This was to fulfill the kind of death that Jesus had said he would suffer.

They also accused him saying, "We found this man leading our nation astray and telling us not to pay our taxes to Caesar and saying that he is Messiah, that is, a king."

"Are you the king of the Jews?" the governor asked Jesus as he stood before him.

"If you say so," said Jesus.

Yet when the chief priests and elders accused him, he wouldn't answer.

"Don't you hear how many things they accuse you of?"

But Jesus would not answer – not even a single charge. This amazed the governor, and he told the chief priests and the crowds, "I find no guilt in this man."

They pressured him saying, "He stirs up the people, teaching all over Judea and from here to Galilee."

When Pilate heard this, he inquired if the man was a Galilean, and learning that he belonged to Herod's jurisdiction, he sent him to Herod who happened to be in Jerusalem at that time. Herod was thrilled to see Jesus. He had wanted to see him for a long time. Having heard about him, he was hoping to see him work a miracle, so he questioned him for a while, but Jesus wouldn't answer him. The inquest continued as the chief priests and the scribes accused him viciously. Also, Herod and his soldiers treated him badly and mocked him. Finally, they dressed him in royal clothes and sent him back to Pilate. And that's when Herod and Pilate became friends – that very day. Before that they hated each other.

Then Pilate went again to his headquarters and called for Jesus and asked him, "Are you the king of the Jews?"

"Do you really want to know, or did others tell you about me?"

"Am I a Jew?" asked Pilate. "Your own people and the chief priests have handed you over to me. What have you done?"

"My kingdom is not of this world," said Jesus. "If my kingdom were of this world, my servants would fight and keep me from being handed over to the Jews. But my kingdom is not of this world."

"So then, you are a king?" Pilate pressed.

"You say I'm a king. For this purpose I was born, and for this purpose I have come into the world – to bear witness to the truth. People who want truth listen to me."

Pilate said, "What is truth?"

Each year at the feast, the governor normally released any one prisoner of the crowd's choosing. At that time, they had a notorious prisoner, a robber named Barabbas. He had been thrown into prison for an insurrection started in the city and for murder.

Pilate called the chief priests, the rulers, and the people and said to them, "You brought me this man, saying he was leading the people astray. But after questioning him in front of you, I didn't find him guilty of any of your charges. Neither did Herod, so he sent him back to us. Look, you can see that he's done nothing deserving death. Instead, I will punish him and let him go."

But they all shouted, "Take this man away and let Barabbas go!"

Pilate wanted to release Jesus. Therefore, he went to them one more time, knowing that they had delivered him up out of envy. Also, while he was sitting on the judgment seat, his wife sent word to him: "Don't have anything to do with that man – he's righteous. Last night I had a bad dream about him."

So Pilate said, "It's customary for me to release one man for you at the Passover. Which one will it be – Barabbas or Jesus who is called Christ? Do you want me to release for you the king of the Jews?"

Yet they kept shouting, "CRUCIFY HIM! CRUCIFY HIM!"

"Why? What evil has he done? I can't find him guilty of anything deserving death. Instead, I will punish him and let him go."

Then Pilate had Jesus scourged. The governor's soldiers took Jesus into the palace (that is the governor's headquarters) and they gathered the whole battalion around him, and they stripped him. Some of the soldiers twisted together a crown of thorns and pressed it into his head, and they adorned him in a purple robe and put a reed in his right hand. Then the mocking really began. They were saluting him and kneeling down before him saying, "Hail, King of the Jews!" as they were slapping him and spitting on him and hitting him over the head with the reed.

Pilate went out again and said to them, "See, I'm bringing him out to you to show you that I find him guilty of nothing. Behold the man!" he said as Jesus came out wearing the crown of thorns and the purple robe.

When the chief priests and the officers saw him, they just kept shouting, "CRUCIFY HIM! CRUCIFY HIM!"

"You take him and you crucify him! I say he's innocent!"

"We have a Law," they demanded, "and according to that Law he ought to die because he declared himself the Son of God."

This statement shook Pilate all the more, and he went back inside again and asked Jesus, "Where are you from?"

Jesus didn't say a word. So Pilate said to him, "You won't answer me? Don't you know that I have the authority to crucify you or to let you go?"

"You have no authority over me at all unless it has been given to you from above. That's why the one who delivered me over to you has the greater sin."

From then on, Pilate tried to find a way to release him, but the Jews kept shouting, "If you let him go, you're no 'friend of Caesar,' and 'everyone who makes himself a king is Caesar's enemy.'"

When Pilate heard this, he brought Jesus out and sat down on the judgment seat at a place called The Stone

Pavement (known as Gabbatha in the Aramaic language). It was about the sixth hour on the Day of Preparation for the Passover.

"Behold your king!" he said to the Jews.

"AWAY WITH HIM!"

"GET HIM OUT OF HERE!"

"CRUCIFY HIM!"

"Do you want me to crucify your king?" Pilate answered.

"WE HAVE NO KING BUT CAESAR!" shouted the chief priests, urging his crucifixion.

Pilate could see that he was getting nowhere and a riot was beginning. Their voices prevailed. Pilate decided to grant them their demand. Then he took water and washed his hands so the crowd could see, saying, "I am innocent of this man's blood. You do this thing yourselves."

And all the people answered, "HIS BLOOD BE ON US AND ON OUR CHILDREN!"

He released the man who had been thrown into prison for insurrection and murder and delivered Jesus over to their will.

They ripped the purple robe off Jesus, put his own clothes back on him and led him away to be crucified.

Crucifixion

[159]Then Jesus went out bearing his own cross. Along the way, they grabbed a man passing by who was just coming in from the country. His name was Simon of Cyrene. He was Alexander and Rufus' father. They laid the cross on him, and he carried it behind Jesus. A large crowd followed him, including the women mourning and lamenting. Jesus turned to the women and said, "Daughters of Jerusalem, don't cry for me; cry for yourselves and for your children. The days are coming when they will say, 'Blessed are the barren and the wombs that never bore and the breasts that never nursed!' Then they'll say to the mountains, 'Fall on us!' and to the hills, 'Cover us!' You see, if they do these things when the wood is green, what will happen when it is dry?"

Two other men, criminals and robbers, were taken out to be put to death with him, and they reached the place called The Skull (known as Golgotha in the Aramaic language) at 9:00 a.m. That's where they crucified Jesus and the criminals, one on his right and one on his left.

"Father, forgive them," Jesus cried, "they don't know what they're doing."

They tried to get him to drink sour wine mixed with gall and myrrh, but when he tasted it, he wouldn't drink it.

Before they crucified him, they took his clothes and divided them into four parts, one part for each soldier. They also took his tunic. It was one seamless piece woven from top to bottom, so they said, "Don't tear it, but let's gamble to see who gets it." This fulfilled the Scripture that says, [160]*They gambled for my clothes.*

---

[159] Mark 15:21-41; Matthew 27:32-56; Luke 23:26-49;
   John 19:17-37
[160] Psalm 22:18

And they sat down and kept watch over him. Pilate had these charges posted over his head: "This is Jesus of Nazareth, the King of the Jews." The place where Jesus was crucified was near the city, and many of the Jews read this inscription, so it was written in Aramaic, Latin, and Greek. But the Jewish chief priest said to Pilate, "Do not write, 'The King of the Jews.' Instead, write, 'This man said I am King of the Jews.'"

"What I have written I have written," Pilate answered.

Meanwhile, some people stood by watching, but others passed by berating him, wagging their heads and saying, "You could destroy the temple and rebuild it in three days, so save yourself!"

"If you're the Son of God, come down from the cross!"

The chief priests, scribes, and elders mocked him as well, saying, "He saved others, but he can't save himself!"

"Well, if he is God's Messiah, his Chosen One, he can save himself!" answered others.

"He's the King of Israel! Now let the Messiah come down from the cross so that we can see it and believe in him."

"He trusts in God, let God deliver him now if he wants him since he said, 'I am the Son of God.'"

The soldiers mocked him too, coming up and offering him sour wine and saying, "If you're the King of the Jews, save yourself!"

Even the robbers who were crucified with Jesus reviled him like the rest.

But standing by the cross of Jesus were his mother and his mother's sister, Mary, the wife of Clopas, and Mary Magdalene. When Jesus saw his mother and the disciple he loved standing close by, he said to her, "Woman, look at your son."

And he said to the disciple, "Look, she's your mother now." Right then the disciple took her as his own.

There were also many other women who came up with him to Jerusalem. These women helped him and followed

169

him from Galilee and now watched from a distance. Among them were Mary, the mother of the younger James, and Joses, and the mother of the sons of Zebedee, and Salome.

One of the criminals hanging there railed at him, "Aren't you the Messiah? Then save yourself and us!"

But the other rebuked him, "Don't you fear God since you're under the same sentence of condemnation? And ours is just. We're getting what we deserve, but this man's done nothing wrong."

Turning to Jesus, he said, "Remember me when you come into your kingdom."

"Truly, I'm telling you," said Jesus, "today you'll be with me in Paradise."

At noon, the sun's light failed and it got dark over the whole land until three o'clock. At that time, Jesus cried out loudly, [161]"*Eli, Eli, lema sabachthani?*" That is, "*My God, my God, why have you forsaken me?*"

When some of the bystanders heard it they said, "He's calling Elijah."

But others said, "Wait! Let's see if Elijah comes to save him."

After this, Jesus knew that everything was finished, and to fulfill Scripture he said, [162]"*I'm thirsty.*"

One of them ran to a jar full of sour wine that was there and filled a sponge and put it on a hyssop branch and gave it to him to drink. When he finished drinking the sour wine, he cried out with a loud voice, "IT IS FINISHED! Father, I put my spirit in your hands!"

And he bowed his head...

and gave up his spirit...

and took his last breath.

In the temple, the veil was ripped in two from top to bottom and the earth shook and rocks split. The graves also

---

[161] Psalm 22:1
[162] Psalm 69:11

opened and many bodies of the saints who had fallen asleep were raised. They came out of the graves after his resurrection and went into the holy city and appeared to many.

When the centurion who stood in front of Jesus and those who were keeping watch over him saw the way he took his last breath and the earthquake and all that occurred, they were filled with awe and said, "This was definitely the Son of God!"

"Certainly this man was innocent!" the centurion exclaimed as he praised God.

And all the crowds that had gathered for this spectacle went home beating their breasts when they saw what had taken place. All of Jesus' acquaintances and the women who had followed him from Galilee were standing farther away, watching.

[163]It was the Day of Preparation, and the Jews didn't want the bodies to remain on the crosses on the Sabbath because that Sabbath was a holy day, so they asked Pilate to have the legs broken and the bodies taken down. The soldiers came and broke the legs of the first man, then the other man who had been crucified with Jesus. When they came to Jesus and saw that he was already dead, they did not break his legs. But one of the soldiers stuck a spear in his side. Immediately, blood and water came out. These things happened to fulfill the Scripture: [164]*Not one of his bones will be broken.* Another Scripture says, [165]*They will look on him whom they have pierced.*

Then a rich man named Joseph came from Arimathea. He was a respected member of the council – a good and righteous man who had not consented to their decision. He was even looking for the kingdom of God, being

---

[163] Mark 15:42-47; Matthew 27:57-66; Luke 23:50-56; John 19:38-42
[164] Exodus 12:46; Numbers 9:12; Psalm 34:20
[165] Zechariah 12:10

a disciple of Jesus, but secretly for fear of the Jews. He boldly went to Pilate and asked for the body of Jesus.

Pilate was surprised to hear that he was already dead. He called for the centurion and asked him to confirm it. The centurion verified that he was dead, so Pilate granted the corpse to Joseph.

Joseph took Jesus down from the cross. Nicodemus, the one who had earlier come to Jesus by night, was with Joseph. Nicodemus brought a mixture of about seventy-five pounds of myrrh and aloes. Together they took the body of Jesus and wrapped it in clean linen cloths with the spices as is the burial custom of the Jews. There was a garden close to where he was crucified. In it was a new tomb belonging to Joseph that he had cut out of the rock. No one had been buried there before, and since it was close by, they laid Jesus there because of the Jewish Day of Preparation. Finally, he rolled a huge stone against the entrance of the tomb and left.

It was now the Day of Preparation and the Sabbath was beginning. Mary Magdalene and Mary the mother of Joses and the women who had come with Jesus from Galilee had followed Joseph. They sat opposite the tomb and saw how his body was laid. Then the women returned and prepared spices and ointments. On the Sabbath, they rested according to the commandment.

The next day, that is, the one after the day of Preparation, the chief priests and the Pharisees went to Pilate and said, "Sir, we remember how that impostor said while he was still alive, 'After three days, I will rise.' Therefore, order the tomb to be made secure until the third day. Otherwise, his disciples may go and steal him away and tell the people, 'He has risen from the dead.' That fraud would be worse than the first."

"You have soldiers," said Pilate. "Go. Make it as secure as you can." So they went and secured the tomb by sealing the stone and setting a guard.

Resurrection

[166]After the Sabbath, near the dawn of the first day of the week, Mary Magdalene, Mary the mother of James, Salome, Joanna, and the other women went to see the tomb. They had bought and prepared spices to take with them to anoint Jesus. They left while it was still dark.

Meanwhile, there had been a serious earthquake because an angel of the Lord, who looked like a young man, descended from Heaven and came and rolled back the stone and sat on it. His appearance was like lightning with clothing white as snow. The guards were so terrified they shook and froze like dead men.

The ladies reached the tomb after the sun had risen. Along the way, they were wondering, "Who's going to roll the stone away from the tomb?" Arriving and looking up, they saw that the stone had already been rolled away, and it was huge.

Mary Magdalene left and ran to Simon Peter and the other disciple, the one whom Jesus loved, and said to them, "They have taken the Lord out of the tomb, and we don't know where they have laid him."

The other women who remained, entered the tomb but did not find the body of the Lord Jesus. While they were perplexed about this, suddenly, two men stood by them — glowing!

The angel, who sat down on the right side, said to the women who were alarmed and had their faces bowed to the ground, "Don't be afraid. Why are you looking for the living among the dead? I know you're looking for Jesus of Nazareth who was crucified. He's not here because he has risen, just like he said. Remember how he told you, while he was still in

---

[166] Mark 16:1-11; Matthew 28:1-15; Luke 24:1-12;
John 20:1-18

Galilee, that the Son of Man must be delivered into the hands of sinful men, be crucified, and rise again on the third day? Here, see the place where they laid him. Then go quickly and tell his disciples that he has risen from the dead – and tell Peter. Tell them that he is going ahead of you to Galilee and you will see him there again just as he told you. See, now I have told you."

The ladies remembered what Jesus had said and left the tomb in a hurry, still afraid but overjoyed, and they said nothing to anyone because of their fear.

Later, Mary returned and stood outside the tomb weeping. As she cried, she stooped to look into the tomb and saw two angels in white, sitting where the body of Jesus had laid, one at the head and one at the feet.

"Woman, why are you crying?" they asked.

"They have taken away my Lord, and I don't know where they laid him," Mary answered. After she said this, she turned around and saw Jesus standing there, but she didn't know that it was Jesus.

"Woman, why are you crying?" Jesus asked. "Who are you looking for?"

Mary thought he was the gardener, so she said, "Sir, if you have moved him, tell me where you laid him, and I will take him away."

"Mary," said Jesus.

She turned. "Rabboni!" she said in Aramaic (which means Teacher).

"Don't hold on to me so tight, for I have not yet ascended to the Father. But go to my brothers and say to them, 'I am ascending to my Father and your Father, to my God and your God.'"

So Jesus first appeared to Mary Magdalene from whom he had cast out seven demons. Then she went to the disciples and told them, as they mourned and wept, "I have seen the Lord! He is alive!" She also told them the things he said to her, but the disciples refused to believe it.

174

And as the other women walked along, Jesus met them and said, "Good morning."

They came up and took hold of his feet and worshiped him. "Don't be afraid," said Jesus, "but go and tell my brothers to go to Galilee where they will see me."

They ran and told all these things to the eleven and also to the rest, but the story seemed like a crazy tale so they didn't believe them.

However, Peter and the other disciple decided to go to the tomb, and while they were on their way, some of the guards went into the city and told the chief priests all that had happened. After they had assembled with the elders and made a plan, they gave enough money to the soldiers and said, "Tell people, 'His disciples came by night and stole him while we were asleep.' And if the governor hears about this, we'll take care of him and keep you out of trouble." So they took the money and did as they were told. That story has been spread among the Jews to this day.

Elsewhere, Peter and the other disciple were running together, but the other disciple outran Peter and reached the tomb first. He bent down to look in, and he saw the linen cloths lying there, but he didn't go in. Then Simon Peter arrived and went into the tomb. He saw the linen cloths lying there and the face cloth that had been on Jesus' head. It wasn't lying with the linen cloths but was folded up in a place by itself. The other disciple, who had reached the tomb first, also went in. He saw it all and he believed. Clearly, they didn't understand the Scriptures that he would rise from the dead. Then the disciples went back to their homes marveling at what had happened.

[167]That same day, two of them were going to a village called Emmaus about seven miles from Jerusalem, and they were talking with each other about all these things that had happened. While they were talking and discussing together,

---

[167] Mark 16:12-14; Luke 24:13-49; Acts 1:4-5; John 20:19-29

Jesus came along and went with them, but their eyes were kept from recognizing him.

"What are you talking about while you walk?" asked Jesus.

They just stood there, looking sad. Then one of them, named Cleopas, answered him, "Are you the only one visiting Jerusalem who doesn't know what's happened there lately?"

"What?" Jesus asked.

They told him, "It's all about Jesus of Nazareth, a man who was a mighty prophet in word and deed before God and everybody and how our chief priests and rulers caused him to be condemned to death and crucified. We had hoped that he was the one who would redeem Israel. Yes, and besides all this, it's been three days since everything happened. Also, some women we know amazed us. They were at the tomb early in the morning and couldn't find his body, and they came back telling us they had seen a vision of angels who said he was alive. Some of those who were with us went to the tomb and confirmed what the women said, but they didn't see Jesus."

And Jesus said, "O how dim-witted and slow of heart to believe all that the prophets have spoken! Was it not necessary for the Messiah to suffer these things and enter into his glory?" Then he began with Moses and all the Prophets and showed them throughout the Scriptures all the things written about him.

As they approached the village where they were going, he acted as if he were continuing on, but they worked hard to persuade him to stay, saying, "You should stay with us. This day is nearly over and it's almost nighttime." So he stayed.

He sat at the table with them and he took the bread and blessed it. As he broke it and gave it to them, their eyes were opened and they recognized him. Then he vanished.

"That's why our hearts were on fire while he talked with us along the road and explained the Scriptures to us," they said to each other. They got up right away and went back to Jerusalem where they found the eleven and all who were with them gathered together. They told them, "The Lord has definitely been raised from the dead! And he has appeared to Simon!"

They described what had happened along the road and how they recognized him when he broke the bread. But they didn't believe them.

Later that evening, the first day of the week, they were talking about it all as they reclined at the table. The doors were locked because they were afraid of the Jews.

"Peace be with you," they heard Jesus say as he came and stood among them.

They were shocked and scared. They thought they were seeing a ghost. "Why are you so shaken, and why all this doubt in your hearts? Look at my hands and my feet...it's me...look...touch me. Spirits don't have flesh and bones as you see I have." He said all this showing them his hands and his side and his feet. They couldn't believe what they were seeing – the excitement was overwhelming.

"Is there anything here to eat?" he asked.

They gave him a piece of broiled fish, and he ate it there in front of them. Later, while staying with them, he ordered them not to leave Jerusalem, but to wait for the Father's promise.

And he rebuked them for their hard hearts and for not believing those who said they saw him after he had risen. "This is what I was talking about while I was still with you," he explained, "that everything written about me in the Law of Moses and the Prophets and the Psalms had to be fulfilled."

Then he opened their minds to understand the Scriptures and said, "This is what is written, that the Messiah should suffer and on the third day rise from the dead, and that repentance and forgiveness of sins should be proclaimed in his name to every people group starting from Jerusalem. You are witnesses to it all. Look, I'm sending you the promise of my Father – John immersed you in water, but not many days from now you will be immersed with the Holy Spirit. Stay in the city until you are clothed with power from on high. Then you will go throughout the world telling this good news to the whole creation. And whoever believes and is immersed will be saved, but those who don't believe will be condemned. The following signs will accompany those who believe in my name: they will cast out demons, speak in new tongues, and pick up snakes by hand. Also, if they drink any deadly poison, it won't hurt them, and they will lay their hands on sick people who will be healed. Peace be with you," he repeated, "just as the Father has sent me, I am sending you."

After he told them these things, he breathed on them and said, "Receive the Holy Spirit. If you forgive the sins of anyone, they are forgiven. If you withhold forgiveness from anyone, it is withheld."

Now Thomas was not with them when Jesus came. He was one of the Twelve and also known as the Twin. The other disciples told him, "We have seen the Lord."

But he said, "Unless I see the nail marks in his hands and stick my finger in them, and put my hand into his side, I will never believe."

Eight days later, Thomas was inside with the disciples. The doors were locked, yet Jesus came and stood in the middle of them and said, "Peace be with you. Thomas, put your finger right here in my hands. Take your hand and put it in my side. Don't doubt anymore – believe."

"My Lord and my God!" Thomas exclaimed.

"You are believing because you've seen me? Blessed are those who have not seen me and believe anyway."

[168]Later, the eleven disciples went to Galilee, to the mountain where Jesus had directed them. When they saw him, they worshiped him, although some doubted. Then Jesus came and said, "All authority in Heaven and on Earth has been given to me. So go, and as you are going, make disciples of all people groups, immersing them in the name of

---

[168] Matthew 28:16-20

the Father, and of the Son, and of the Holy Spirit, teaching them to do all that I have commanded you. And oh yes, I will always be with you…to the end of the age."

[169]After this, Jesus revealed himself again to the disciples by the Sea of Tiberias. It happened this way: Simon Peter, Thomas (called the Twin), Nathanael of Cana in Galilee, Zebedee's sons, and two other disciples were together.

Simon Peter said, "I'm going fishing."

"We'll go with you," said the others.

They got in the boat, went out, and caught nothing all night. Right at daybreak, Jesus stood on the shore, but the disciples didn't know it was Jesus.

"Boys, catch any fish?"

"No."

"Cast the net on the right side of the boat. That's where you'll find them."

They did, and they couldn't pull the net in because there were too many fish.

Then the disciple Jesus loved said to Peter, "It's the Lord!"

When Simon Peter heard that, he put on his outer clothes since he was nearly naked and dove into the sea.

The other disciples came in the boat, dragging the net full of fish. They weren't far from shore, only about a hundred yards out. When they got to land, they saw a charcoal fire with fish laid out on it along with bread.

"Bring some of the fish that you caught," Jesus said.

So Simon Peter went on board and pulled the net full of 153 fish up on the shore. And even though there were so many fish, the net wasn't torn.

"Come and have breakfast," invited Jesus.

Not one of the disciples even dared to ask, "Who are you?" They knew it was the Lord.

---

[169] John 21:1-23

Jesus picked up the bread and gave it to them. He also gave them the fish. This was now the third time that Jesus was revealed to the disciples after he was raised from the dead.

After breakfast, Jesus said to Simon Peter, "Simon, son of John, do you love me more than they do?"

"Yes Lord, you know that I love you," he answered.

"Then feed my lambs," Jesus told him.

"Simon, son of John, do you love me?" he asked again.

"Yes Lord, you know that I love you," Peter repeated.

"Then tend my sheep," said Jesus.

"Simon, son of John, do you love me?" he continued to ask for a third time.

This third "Do you love me?" really hurt Peter inside. He answered, "Lord, you know everything. You know that I love you."

"Then feed my sheep. The truth is – when you were young, you used to dress yourself and walk wherever you wanted. But when you are old, you will stretch out your hands while others dress you and carry you where you do not want to go." (Jesus said this to show the kind of death Peter would die to glorify God.) After that Jesus said, "Follow me."

Peter turned and saw the disciple Jesus loved following them. (He was the one who had been reclining at the table close to him and had asked, "Lord, who is going to betray you?")

When Peter saw him, he said to Jesus, "Lord, what about him?"

"What's it to you? Even if I want him to stay until I come – you follow me."

As a result, the saying spread out among the brothers that this disciple wouldn't die. But Jesus didn't say he wouldn't die, he said, "Even if I want him to stay until I come, what's that to you?"

[170]Later, when they had gathered, Jesus led them out as far as Bethany, and they asked him, "Lord, now will you restore the kingdom to Israel?"

He lifted up his hands and blessed them. "It's not for you to know the times or seasons that the Father has fixed by his own authority. But you'll receive power when the Holy Spirit has come on you, and you'll be my witnesses in Jerusalem, and in all Judea and Samaria, and to the ends of the earth."

After saying these things, they were watching as he was lifted up and a cloud took him out of their sight. Then he sat down at the right hand of God. They stood staring into Heaven as he went, when suddenly, two men in white robes stood beside them and said, "Men of Galilee, why are you standing here staring at Heaven? This same Jesus, who was taken up from you into Heaven, will come back in the same way you saw him go."

They worshiped Jesus, ecstatic as they returned to Jerusalem. And they were continually in the temple blessing God. Afterward, they went and preached everywhere as Jesus worked with them and confirmed the message through miraculous signs.

---

[170] Mark 16:15-20; Luke 24:50-53; Acts 1:6-11

P.S.

[171]This is the disciple who says he witnessed these things and wrote them down. And we know that his testimony is true – so that you also may believe.

There are many other things that Jesus did. If every one of them were written down, I don't suppose the world could hold the books that would be written.

Jesus did many other signs in the presence of the disciples which are not written in this book. But these are written so you may believe that Jesus is

...the Messiah

...the Son of God.

If you believe...you can have life in his name.

---

[171] John 21:24-25; 20:30-31

Family Tree

[172]When Jesus began his ministry, he was about thirty years old. He was the son (so they thought) of Joseph, the son of Heli, the son of Matthat, the son of Levi, the son of Melchi, the son of Jannai, the son of Joseph, the son of Mattathias, the son of Amos, the son of Nahum, the son of Esli, the son of Naggai, the son of Maath, the son of Mattathias, the son of Semein, the son of Josech, the son of Joda, the son of Joanan, the son of Rhesa, the son of Zerubbabel, the son of Shealtiel, the son of Neri, the son of Melchi, the son of Addi, the son of Cosam, the son of Elmadam, the son of Er, the son of Joshua, the son of Eliezer, the son of Jorim, the son of Matthat, the son of Levi, the son of Simeon, the son of Judah, the son of Joseph, the son of Jonam, the son of Eliakim, the son of Melea, the son of Menna, the son of Mattatha, the son of Nathan, the son of David, the son of Jesse, the son of Obed, the son of Boaz, the son of Sala, the son of Nahshon, the son of Amminadab, the son of Admin, the son of Arni, the son of Hezron, the son of Perez, the son of Judah, the son of Jacob, the son of Isaac, the son of Abraham, the son of Terah, the son of Nahor, the son of Serug, the son of Reu, the son of Peleg, the son of Eber, the son of Shelah, the son of Cainan, the son of Arphaxad, the son of Shem, the son of Noah, the son of Lamech, the son of Methuselah, the son of Enoch, the son of Jared, the son of Mahalaleel, the son of Cainan, the son of Enos, the son of Seth, the son of Adam, the son of God.

This is the book of the genealogy of Jesus Christ, the son of David, the son of Abraham. Abraham was the father of Isaac, and Isaac the father of Jacob, and Jacob the father of Judah and his brothers, and Judah the father of Perez and Zerah by Tamar, and Perez the father of Hezron, and Hezron

---

[172] Matthew 1:1-17; Luke 3:23-38

the father of Ram, and Ram the father of Amminadab, and Amminadab the father of Nahshon, and Nahshon the father of Salmon, and Salmon the father of Boaz by Rahab, and Boaz the father of Obed by Ruth, and Obed the father of Jesse, and Jesse the father of David the king. David was the father of Solomon by the wife of Uriah, and Solomon the father of Rehoboam, and Rehoboam the father of Abijah, and Abijah the father of Asaph, and Asaph the father of Jehoshaphat, and Jehoshaphat the father of Joram, and Joram the father of Uzziah, and Uzziah the father of Jotham, and Jotham the father of Ahaz, and Ahaz the father of Hezekiah, and Hezekiah the father of Manasseh, and Manasseh the father of Amos, and Amos the father of Josiah, and Josiah the father of Jechoniah and his brothers, at the time of the deportation to Babylon.

After the deportation to Babylon, Jechoniah was the father of Shealtiel, and Shealtiel the father of Zerubbabel, and Zerubbabel the father of Abiud, and Abiud the father of Eliakim, and Eliakim the father of Azor, and Azor the father of Zadok, and Zadok the father of Achim, and Achim the father of Eliud, and Eliud the father of Eleazar, and Eleazar the father of Matthan, and Matthan the father of Jacob, and Jacob the father of Joseph who was the husband of Mary of whom Jesus was born. Jesus is called Messiah. So there are fourteen generations from Abraham to David, and fourteen from David to the deportation to Babylon, and fourteen from the deportation to Messiah.

Questions Considered

Here I have tried to anticipate some of the questions you may have about *Epic*. Whenever you see "I" it refers to Brad, and "we" means Brad and Ann.

Do you claim inspiration for this work?

No. I mean, I was inspired, but I am not claiming inspiration the way many Christians believe the Bible is inspired. Therefore, it's ok to argue that we missed something or that we are wrong. Just be nice.

How is this different from other harmonies and chronologies?

I have purchased every harmony I can find, at least the ones that try to look like a narrative and are not in columns. Of the relatively few in existence, some are complicated with all kinds of numbers and letters trying to give other information or include the editors' commentaries as well. *Epic* contains nothing but the story, no commentary.

Of epic importance is the fact that I left nothing out of any story. What I have found to be an easy litmus test for comparison is the story of Jesus encountering the demoniacs in Gerasa. Most harmonies exclude Matthew's record of two demoniacs. Instead, they defer to Luke and Mark's accounts, which contain only one demoniac. At most, they will footnote that Matthew says there were two. But this omission casts doubt on Matthew's account.

Epic works from the principle that everything found in all four Gospels is true. Therefore, no statement and/or detail in any Gospel may be omitted. This forced me to reconcile every story and present it in a reasonable manner that would work within our time-space continuum.

What is your translation model?

That is a mixed bag, including more literal expressions that are word-for-word and other thought-for-thought wording as in dynamic equivalence. Some will read *Epic* and conclude that it is a paraphrase. The truth is somewhere between our strict understanding of a translation and a paraphrase. On the side of translation, I will argue that we have carefully communicated what is written from the gospels. Yet, I understand the paraphrase label since we didn't translate every word and include it. (More on that in a bit.)

Our serious attempt has been to fully engage every word and phrase in the Gospels, harmonizing them so that nothing is lost in regard to any truth or detail of what each author has given us. We have labored to deliver a translation true to the way people in America communicate today. While some southern colloquialisms may come through, we tried to make it as widely readable as possible.

We felt free to leave out nonessential communication in order to achieve the feel of reading a novel. This is most apparent in dialogue. "And he said to them" is shortened to "he said" and sometimes dropped altogether when the speaker is clear. This type of incidental omission has no bearing whatsoever on the truth, but is critical for creating and maintaining a captivating reading flow.

In addition, verb tenses are not strictly translated, which I am sure will drive Greek technicians crazy. Again, this was an effort to focus on the communication of the text, not a specific verb tense. I fully realize the interpretive license taken in this decision, and will be interested in anyone's demonstrating how any truth was compromised.

Did you add anything?

As absolutely little as possible. On occasion between paragraphs something like a "meanwhile" was added for ease of reading. Also, in the accounts of the servant girls who identify Peter in the courtyard, the word "another" was added

186

to provide distinction between the two different servant girls. So it reads, "and another servant girl saw him." Other than examples of smoothing language such as these, nothing has been added or taken away.

Can we really create a chronology of Christ's life?

After six years of intense research, and consulting more than fifteen chronologies, I would say we can come reasonably close. However, no one can prove that their chronology is certainly the order of every event – there is simply not enough data to support a claim like this. But I do endeavor to get as close as the evidence will allow. This is why I use the term "viable chronology" – it could have happened in this order. If you look at chronologies, you will see that there is a wide consensus on the overall progression of events, with disagreement over some of the particulars. In subsequent years, I hope to publish the commentary that will also defend this chronology.

What about the colors in the electronic version?

The serious reader will find value in being able to quickly identify what is uniquely added by each gospel author. Matthew is blue, Mark is orange, Luke is green, and John is purple. The words in their respective color were only recorded by that author. Where two or more gospels say the same thing, the color black is used. And you don't have to remember it all. Each footnote is color-coded for you, allowing you to click a footnote link and be able to see the Bible passages referenced in a given section and which authors contributed to the text in that section.

For more information please visit the website bradandjayme.com. Feel free to ask questions.

32 Picking grain on the Sabbath	12:1-8	2:23-28	6:1-5	
33 Heals withered hand on Sabbath	12:9-14	3:1-6	6:6-11	
34 **By Sea,** third call to Peter		3:9-12	5:1-11	
36 **Chooses the 12 Apostles,** *Sermon on the Mount*	10:2-4 5:1-7:29	3:13-19	6:12-49	
44 **Capernaum**	8:5		7:1	
44 Heals Centurion's Servant	8:5-13		7:1-10	
45 **Town – Nain,** raises dead man			7:11-17	
45 John in prison questions Jesus	11:2-6		7:18-24	
45 Jesus praises John but not crowd	11:7-19		7:25-35	
46 *Woes on cities*	11:20-24			
46 Woman washes Christ's feet			7:36-50	
47 Women who followed Jesus			8:1-3	
48 **Capernaum (home)**				
50 Blind, mute, demonized man healed; *blasphemy against Spirit, sign of Jonah, lamp on a stand*	12:22-50	3:20-35	11:14-36	
50 Family tries intervention			8:19-21	
51 Teaches **by Sea,** *Sower Parable*	13:1-30	4:1-20	8:4-15	
52 *Kingdom Parables – lamp, weeds, mustard seed, yeast, treasure, pearl, net*	13:31-52	4:21-34	8:16-18	
55 Jesus Calms the Sea	13:53, 8:18-27	4:35-41	8:22-25, 9:57-62	
56 **Gerasa/Gadara** heals demoniacs	8:28-34	5:1-20	8:26-39	
57 **Capernaum** Question on fasting	9:14-17	2:18-22	5:33-39	
58 Bleeding woman touches hem, Jairus' daughter healed	9:18-26	5:21-43	8:40-56	
60 Two blind men, demonized mute, "the harvest is full"	9:27-38			
60 Rejected **at Nazareth**	13:54-58	6:1-6	4:16-30	
62 Disciples sent 2 by 2	10:1, 5-11:1	6:7-13	9:1-6	
65 Herod beheads John	14:1-12	6:14-29	9:7-9	
67 **Bethsaida,** Passover 5000 are fed	14:13-22	6:30-45	9:10-17	6:1-15
67 Jesus walks on water, **Gennesaret**	14:23-36	6:46-56		6:16-21
69 **Capernaum,** *Bread of Life*				6:22-71
71 Traditions of Men	15:1-20	7:1-23		
73 **Tyre,** Canaanite woman	15:21-28	7:24-30		
74 **Sidon & Decapolis**, healing and feeding 4000 men	15:29-39	7:31-8:10		
75 **Dalmanutha & Magadan** Pharisees demand signs, beware of leaven of Pharisees	16:1-12	8:11-26		
76 **Bethsaida**, blind man		8:22-26		
77 **Caesarea Philippi,** Peter's confession & rebuke,	16:13-23	8:27-33	9:18-22	
78 take up your cross	16:24-28	8:34-9:1	9:23-27	
78 Transfiguration, *1st Son of Man must die*	17:1-13	9:2-13	9:28-36	
79 heals Epileptic boy	17:14-21	9:14-29	9:37-43	
80 *2nd "Son of Man must die"*	17:22-23	9:30-32	9:44-45	

80 around **Galilee then to Jerusalem** for Feast of Booths				7:1-9 7:10-53
85 *"Your father the Devil, the truth will set you free*				8:1-59
86 Man born blind				9:1-41
89 *The Good Shepherd, The Thief*				10:1-21
90 Feast of **Dedication in Jerusalem**, Jesus nearly stoned by Jews				10:22-39
91 **Capernaum,** *Taxes, Who is the greatest? Children, Temptations, 99 and 1 lost sheep, When your brother sins*	17:24-18:35	9:33-50	9:46-50	
95 **Samaritan** Town rejects Jesus			9:51-56	
95 10 Lepers			17:11-19	
95 **Judea beyond the Jordan**	19:1-2	10:1	10:40-42	
96 72 sent out and *Woes on cities*				10:1-20
97 *I give you rest,* Good Samaritan	11:25-30		10:21-37	
98 **Bethany** at Mary & Martha's			10:38-42	
98 *Teach us to pray*			11:1-13	
99 Pharisees and handwashing			11:37-53	
100 *Fear God, Rich toward God don't worry, Wise manager, be ready...*			12:1-13:9	
104 crippled woman, kingdom parable			13:10-21	
105 through towns and villages, *The narrow door*			13:22-30	
106 *threats, "Jerusalem, Jerusalem"*	23:37-39		13:31-35	
106 "Can we heal on Sabbath?" *Best seats and great feasts Consider the cost*			14:1-35	
108 Parables: Sheep, Coin, Prodigal			15:1-32	
110 Shrewd Manager, Rich man and Lazarus			16:1-17, 19-31	
112 Temptations, Forgive others			17:1-10	
112 Lazarus **in Bethany then a town in Ephraim**			11:1-57	
116 *Signs of coming Kingdom*			17:20-37	
117 *Pray always, Pharisee and Tax Collector*			18:1-14	
117 *Divorce*	19:3-12	10:2-12	16:18	
118 Children, Rich Ruler, Disciples honored on 12 thrones	19:13-30	10:13-31	18:15-30	
120 on the **way to Jerusalem** 3rd *"Son of Man must die,"* James and John's request,	20:17-28	10:32-45	18:31-34	
123 **Jericho**, blind Bartimaeus, Zaccheus, *talents parable*	20:29-34	10:46-52	19:1-27 18:35-43	
123 **Bethany**, Mary anoints Jesus	26:6-13	14:3-9		12:1-11
125 **Mt Olive, Bethpage, Bethany, Triumphal Entry into Jerusalem**	21:1-11	11:1-11	19:28-44	12:1-19
127 Greeks seek Jesus, voice from Heaven, "who has believed"				12:20-50

128 **To Bethany, then Jerusalem** Fig Tree Cursed, Sellers driven from Temple, **back to Bethany**	21:12-22	11:12-26	19:45-48	
130 **Jerusalem**, Pharisees question	21:23-27	11:27-33	20:1-8	
130 *Parables: 2 Sons, Tenants*	21:28-46	12:1-12	20:9-18	
131 *King's Banquet Party*	22:1-14			
132 *Taxes, Woman with 7 husbands*	22:15-33	12:13-27	20:19-40	
134 *Greatest Commandment*	22:34-40	12:28-34		
136 *Woes on Pharisees*	22:41- 23:36	12:35-40	20:41-47	
137 *Widow's Penny*		12:41-44	21:1-4	
138 *Signs of Christ's Return*	24:1-44	13:1-37	21:5-36	
141 *Faithful Servants, Wise Virgins,* *Talents, Sheep and Goats*	24:45- 25:46			
144 **Temple by Day, Olivet by night** Judas makes his deal,	26:1-5, 14-19	14:1,2 10-16	21:37- 22:13	
146 **The Upper Room** and last supper, foot washing, Judas leaves, Lord's supper	26:20-29	14:17-25	22:14-30	13:1-32
149 *New commandment, the way, the* *truth, the life, if you love me*				13:33- 14:31
151 *Vine and branches, Holy Spirit*				15:1-27
152 *Persecution, Holy Spirit, Ask...*				16:1-33
155 *Jesus Prays*				17:1-26
157 **Cross Kidron to Gethsemane** Peter will deny	26:30-35	14:26-31	22:31-34	
159 Swords, In the Garden	26:36-46	14:32-42	22:35-46	18:1
159 Judas' Kiss and Arrest	27:47-56	14:43-52	22:47-53	18:2-11
160 **Before Annas and Caiaphas**, Peter's denial	26:58, 69-75	14:54, 66-72	22:54-65	18:12-27
162 Accused of Blasphemy for claiming to be God	26:57-68	14:53, 55-65	22:63-71	
163 Judas' Remorse and Suicide	27:3-10			
163 **Before Pilate**, Scourged	27:1, 11-31	15:1-20	23:1-25	18:33- 19:16
168 **Crucifixion at Golgotha**	27:32-56	15:21-41	23:26-49	19:17-37
171 Burial and Guard **at Tomb**	27:57-66	15:42-47	23:50-56	19:38-42
173 Resurrection	28:1-15	16:1-11	24:1-12	20:1-18
175 Road to Emmaus		16:12-13	24:13-35	
178 Appears to Disciples **in Galilee**		16:14	24:36-49	20:19-29
178 Great Commission **on mountain** in Galilee				28:16-20
179 Peter and Jesus **by the sea**				21:1-23
181 Ascension **at Bethany**		16:15-20	24:50-53 Acts1:6f	
182 *John's purpose*				21:24-25 20:30-31
188 Family Tree	1:1-17		3:23-38	

Made in the USA
Lexington, KY
26 December 2015